BEHIND
THE WHEEL

*Driving Excellence in
Staffing Operations*

Charted Path Learning Series
A Division of Cleland Consulting Group, LLC d/b/a Charted Path
Suwanee, GA

Designed by Carrie Wallace Brown
Literary Guidance by Bonnie B. Daneker at Write Advisors

Manufactured in the United States of America

ISBN: 978-1-939753-02-1
Library of Congress Control Number: 2013942732

Cleland, Mike
Behind the Wheel: Driving Excellence in Staffing Operations
1. Leadership 2. Organizational Change 3. Influence (Psychology)
4. Industrial Organization 5. Strategic Planning 6. Staffing Operations
7. Management   8. Sales 9. Recruiting

To Staffing Professionals
Dedicated to Mastering Their Craft

Preface

I have met hundreds of people in the staffing industry, and there is one thing they all have in common: they did not plan on entering this business; rather, the staffing business found them. One cannot major in staffing in college or even in graduate school. Instead, people stumble across this industry, and simply fall in love with it.

I am one of those people. I was a pre-med major in college then decided not to go to medical school since it became clear that I lacked the passion and focus to commit to ten more years of schooling. So what does one do with a degree in biology, and hundreds of hours of lab work under one's belt? There are not a lot of options. When the opportunity to become a contractor for the federal government landed in front of me, I took it with great enthusiasm. I would be putting my major to work by studying the health effects of toxic waste sites. I would have job security and a low stress work environment, working 7 a.m. - 4 p.m. with 2 fifteen-minute breaks and a half-hour lunch.

My enthusiasm was relatively short-lived when it became clear that tenure, politics, and subject matter expertise trumped innovation and hard work. I quickly came to realize that I wanted some specific "attainables" from my chosen career. First, I needed to be rewarded based on merit. Second, I needed an industry that would continually challenge me. Third, I needed to work with people who exhibit a passion for what they do.

After a couple years of analyzing health data while sitting in a cubical, a friend of mine introduced me to the world of staffing, and I came to realize that this was an industry I could throw myself into.

In the summer of 1994, I began to go through the newspaper want ads and wrote down the name of every staffing company that was posting positions. For those Generation Y readers, back in those days that is how staffing companies found talent. The "world wide web" was in its infancy and had no great resources for finding a job. I called all the companies to ask if they were hiring recruiters and began the interview process. After interviewing with multiple companies with mixed results, I found the one I wanted. It was a small IT staffing company in a drab office building—complete with a dirty fish tank and wires hanging from the ceiling. It was by far the smallest company that I interviewed with, but I knew this company was going places. The owner was passionate about the business, and had the energy and experience to make her vision a reality.

The only problem was that they were not hiring! But the owner never told me "no", so I kept calling and speaking with her and the senior recruiter, and each time they would ask me to wait a little bit longer. Finally, I decided just to show up at the office and ask for the job in person. It seems aggressive persistence is what they wanted and it was at that point they decided to hire me. I started September 6, 1994. Without a doubt, joining this company was the most important event of my professional career.

My recruiting career lasted close to four years, with mixed results especially in my latter years. After years of additional experience I now understand why my performance lagged: I have a compulsion to always experience new challenges. After a couple years in recruiting, the newness had worn off and I needed something different. Fortunately the company was growing rapidly, and the owner believed I had management potential, so they sent me off to open the first remote office.

My first foray into management was in 1998. It was the peak of the boom in IT staffing with Y2K ramping up to full gear. I moved out of state to open the first branch office. Armed with a budget, three computers and two new-hires with no experience in the industry, I was officially in management. While there was strong financial and moral support from executive management, there was no formal management training. It was a quintessential baptism by fire.

In my first management experience I played the role of sales manager, recruiting manager, IT support, furniture assembler, HR, and general problem solver. It was a time of complete uncertainty, but also one of excitement as I learned more about my talents and limitations in six months than I had in four years in a production role. Stressful? Yes, but stress, hard work, and uncertainty are the tolls we pay for professional development. While I do look back on my first management job as a success, I doubt in today's hyper-competitive market my journey would have been as easy or as positive.

Over the next decade, I was promoted several times and then named President of the $60 million IT division in 2007. During my first few years as President, we had to redefine the sales strategy due to pricing pressures from our largest clients as well as impacts from the recession. Changing the sales strategy is one of the most difficult improvements a staffing company can make and took us over a year to see the desired results. With the improvements to the sales strategy in place, we were able to increase margins, diversify accounts and increase job order volume.

After much soul-searching and gathering of opinions from those whom I respect both professionally and personally, I formed Charted Path in February of 2010. I started Charted Path because I wanted to use my experience as a producer, manager, and executive to provide insight into managing a staffing company. In the last three years I have worked with over 45 different staffing firms from light industrial to high-end IT, ranging from $10 million to $250 million.

This book represents the foundation of what I have learned over the last 19 years. I wanted to write a book that reaches beyond management theory that you see in typical business books and dives into practical application. My initial intent was to write a single book, but it became clear that the topics require greater attention than one book could provide. So instead, this is the first of three books, and focuses on introducing the drivers of high-performance staffing operations.

Many people will ask if these books are really necessary since staffing at its heart is entrepreneurial in nature and is not much for formality and structure. For those people I would argue that the job of managing a staffing company is getting harder year after year and this book is an important resource to empower current and future leaders to manage successfully in spite of an increasingly difficult marketplace.

For a staffing manger to be effective in today's marketplace, the person must be well informed, passionate, and willing to make difficult decisions. One of the biggest mistakes I see staffing executives make is underestimating the skills and importance of a strong staffing manager. My focus on the importance and difficulty of staffing management may just be based on personal bias; however, I have seen experienced managers from other industries come to staffing and quickly become shell-shocked. The staffing business may be easy to understand, but it is very difficult to effectively execute. My hope is in reading this book you will find the tools you need to enhance both your management experience and effectiveness.

Mike Cleland
President, Charted Path

Foreword

The staffing industry is simple to understand, but difficult to master. Basically, staffing is people helping people find people. It is that simple. Within this definition, though, lies the difficulty. People have diverse needs, wants, drivers and goals. As such, mastering the skill to bring people together requires the ability to navigate the ever-changing tide of human behavior. This complexity multiplies when you add the needs of other people involved in a successful placement – spouses, friends, family, peers, co-workers, bosses, and now social media sites, such as glassdoor.com.

This industry started as a relationship business and relationships will continue to influence its success. Beyond relationships are other equally important success factors. One of the most essential factors is the ability to have excellent execution in your business operations. The fulfillment portion of the staffing industry is similar to a supply chain where the quality and quantity of input (job requisitions and candidate profiles) along with the productivity of effort (submittals and interviews) determine the output (deals and starts). Leading staffing companies have strong management teams that maximize the productive output of their operations, while holding firmly to the basics of this being a business of, for and by the people.

This is what *Behind the Wheel* addresses and where Mike Cleland excels. I have had the privilege of knowing Mike for 19 years and am proud to call him a colleague and a friend. We have been co-workers and my company has engaged his consulting services. We both started our careers with a small IT staffing firm in Georgia – where Mike was a Recruiter and I was an Account Manager. Over time we both grew into leadership roles: from opening new branch offices, to running larger offices, becoming Directors and ultimately Executives within the company. We both started at the desk and we understand the importance of establishing streamlined operations in which passionate professionals with a strong work ethic can succeed. Mike's organization, Charted Path, knows what it takes to make this a reality and can help your company attain it.

Mike's first executive role in our former company was as Vice President of Operations. In this capacity he coached his management team, streamlined processes and aligned tools in a manner that enabled our team members to more easily understand and excel in our operations. He was then promoted to President, and his ability to enhance a culture of trust, respect and going the extra mile rounded out the operational strength he helped build. As President, his understanding of management's role in driving staffing operations and his own ability to trouble shoot business problems were best put to use and refined.

Mike thrives on coaching and developing a management team to help them turnaround underperforming—and sometimes broken—operations, while simultaneously educating them on how staffing operations should work. This drive is what led him to pursue his own consulting business in 2010.

When I joined Randstad Engineering in January 2010 as Vice President of Sales, an area of immediate focus was the evaluation of our existing sales strategy. Randstad Engineering (U.S.) is an operating company of Randstad, a $22.5 billion global provider of Human Resources Services and the second largest staffing organization in the world. Our Executive Management team realized an opportunity to drive growth through productivity improvement, specifically our job order conversion ratio and our submittal-to-hire ratio. We engaged Charted Path to assist us with the analysis work to identify key issues.

The experience with Mike was both productive and revealing. We have a strong management team, but Mike challenged important assumptions and changed critical perceptions on how we should manage the business. The end result was a streamlined approach that increased results by over 40% with nominal SG&A investment.

If you are a manager, executive or owner of a staffing organization and you recognize the opportunity to improve the operations of your organization, then this book is for you. You will learn the drivers that need to be managed in a staffing operation and how they can be improved to increase competitiveness. If you choose to engage Charted Path, then you will benefit by having a proven professional assist you in troubleshooting your team's primary performance issues, facilitating solutions with your team to drive acceptance, and providing you with ongoing management coaching as changes are implemented. All in all, a solid return on your investment.

David Findley, Vice President of Sales
Randstad Engineering (U.S.), February 2013

Contents

Contents

Introduction

Staffing managers of even the most successful staffing companies recognize that there is no room for unbridled optimism. The staffing industry faces headwinds that are driven from multiple forces beyond its direct control. Clients continue to ask for more while paying less. New regulations and stronger enforcement of existing regulations increase the cost of doing business. The changing face of technology challenges how we must leverage the talent pool, which is the very essence of our service. Complicating all of these challenges is recognizing that economic growth is inconsistent and unstable. All these factors mandate that staffing companies develop strong managers who can rise above the inertia of the status quo and develop and implement high-impact operational improvements to keep up with the rising challenges and ensure long-term sustainability.

My intent is to provide you an introduction to the drivers in a contract staffing company so that you can more effectively define and manage the company strategy and identify high impact improvements within the organization. We will talk in generalities: this book is not going to provide specific solutions. Company circumstances are different, and every solution must be customized to meet the needs of each specific situation. Managers should embrace this complexity because if solutions could be turn-key, there would be no need for management. Becoming familiar with the terms in this book will enhance your communication with your teams, your superiors, and your peers in the industry. For your reference, there is a Glossary in the back of the book.

We will spend some time throughout the book discussing how the concepts of these drivers can be applied to your business today, but by no means are those applications meant to be universal or comprehensive. Specifically, Chapter 5 provides some guidance and questions to get you started. Great managers are creative problem solvers and apply solutions that best fit their circumstances. Learning how to adjust their management approach and push improvement through these drivers is where staffing managers will see the most return from this book.

We welcome your questions and suggestions. Please feel free to email me at questions@chartedpath.com.

Chapter 1: The Goal

Change is accelerating everywhere and is driven by a combination of technology, demographics, and even geopolitical forces. Anyone who pays attention to market trends understands the threats and opportunities associated with change. As leaders, we must learn to accept its inevitability and adapt our organizations. To do otherwise is to abdicate our role and leave the survival of our organizations simply to chance.

Over the last 25 years, staffing companies have had to maneuver through bursting market bubbles, more educated buyers, and rapidly changing technologies. No one knows what the next set of challenges will look like. All we do know is that those challenges are coming and only companies with managers who are capable of adapting their operations will thrive. These organizations will continue to strengthen company competitiveness through focused strategies and an innovative management team striving for operational excellence. Executives and managers who put their hope in the status quo are trusting that nothing will change, though history proves otherwise.

As a staffing manager, you have undoubtedly seen that staffing performance drivers lead to strong financial results. You also know that you need to understand them to manage effectively. In this book, we will provide an introduction to these drivers as the critical components of an overall management framework. This framework helps you both better define your role as a manager and gives you the insight you need to execute your company's strategy.

There may be executives and managers out there who think a formal management framework overcomplicates the business. On the contrary, formal management procedures empower management decision making in three ways:

1. **Greater Situational Awareness:** Understanding all the variables that could be impacting productivity helps managers identify bottlenecks. This comprehensive approach to problem solving is critical in ensuring that the management team focuses its energy on the right challenge. A common mistake managers make is to concentrate on problems that are immediate and highly visible, assuming they are the most critical. This is a serious misstep.

   Often, the problems that are the true performance bottlenecks within an operation have been brewing beneath the surface for some time. Ensuring all drivers are effectively evaluated also addresses the problems of solution bias. Solution bias occurs when a manager continually makes the same assumptions regarding the reasons for performance issues. These assumptions are frequently hard-coded by a combination of experience and business philosophy. For example, a sales manager may assume job order close rates are always due to candidate quality issues, since in a previous job he worked with a junior-level recruiting team. However, there are many potential variables that impact job order close rate, including job order quality and responsiveness. Solution bias limits the manager's thinking to the point where he is unable to evaluate all the variables influencing performance.

2. **More Effective Communication:** Thoroughly identifying and defining all drivers captures all critical functions, therefore enabling effective analysis and problem solving. Precise language is required for precise thinking. I have witnessed this impact while coaching managers. When using more precise language, the managers' view of the business changes. Most experienced managers know that these concepts exist, but without the appropriate language they struggle to develop and communicate their thoughts.

   This becomes especially significant when an organization grows past the $20 million range. At that point the operations become more complex and making decisions based on "gut feelings" begins to lose effectiveness. Furthermore, at this point most companies hire additional managers. Now the operational knowledge is divided among more leaders. These leaders need clear language to update each other and to collaborate on the increasingly complex problems their company faces. This inability to communicate not only undermines collaboration, but also can compromise the trust between managers, generating long-term damage to their professional relationship.

3. **Well-Aligned Metrics Portfolio:** Building awareness of these drivers builds a framework for a metric system that gives managers the visibil-

ity they need to make the right decisions. When I evaluate metric systems of various companies, I discover that they suffer from a number of problems, including quantity, quality, and proper balance.

The Management Framework

A few years ago, I was attending a workshop on the Kaplan and Norton management system, which is excellent when properly applied. Every approach has unintended consequences and this became abundantly clear when speaking to a fellow workshop attendee.

"Susan" was very bright, but had no real experience in management. She worked for a government agency that was in the process of implementing the system. When I asked her how she was enjoying the class, she told me how exciting it was to learn that holding different divisions accountable would keep them focused on what is important. Now, this is a perfectly reasonable take-away, but it was not what she said but how she said it that concerned me. It was clear by her tone that she saw the management system as the ultimate wisdom of the operations. It provided the rules; the people just needed to comply.

Experienced managers understand that this narrow thinking undermines a management system's very purpose. Managers use a system to give themselves structure, but they need to apply discernment and make the right calls. Good managers understand that there are no rules, only judgments. The real question is whether that judgment is well-informed.

To drive effective innovation, managers need a fundamental framework that establishes a direction, provides visibility, and drives accountability. This type of disciplined framework is rare in the staffing industry today for some very specific reasons. In order to appreciate the importance of focus and discipline in implementing a strong management framework, it is important to understand why these frameworks are most commonly resisted in the industry:

Entrepreneurial Culture: The staffing industry is entrepreneurial and sales driven. These factors contribute to a management culture that is skeptical of formal management approaches. Instead, an entrepreneurial culture leans on strong leadership and individual producers to drive growth. This can work to a point. There are plenty of $10 million to $20 million staffing companies that are very informally managed. Eventually, those companies will struggle to drive organic growth as competitive forces increase, and the companies' inefficiencies develop into bottlenecks.

People-Focused: Staffing is about people, and because of this managers tend to see business problems solely as people problems. Revamping the strategy, processes, and management approaches seem alien to many staffing managers. Instead, they tend to focus on the effectiveness of individual managers and producers, as well as organizational structure. While focusing on personnel is important, too often it blinds management to other sources of performance bottlenecks.

Lack of Language: Have you engaged in a heated discussion with someone only to find out later that the one thing you really disagree on is the meaning of the words you are using? Without clear language you cannot clearly define the problems or collaborate effectively to address those problems. A few years ago, I got into a lengthy discussion with a marketing consultant on how best to manage leads. The conversation went on for several minutes until I realized she defined a lead as a company, while I defined it as an opportunity. Once we were on the same page, we could collaborate on a solution. Most staffing managers lack the vocabulary to discuss the problems they face. This leads to muddled thinking and ineffective collaboration. Clear language allows for clear problem solving.

A management framework addresses these issues by providing the management team with the information and the discipline required to make the right decisions. The days of "gut-feel" are replaced with an informed intuition that has a balanced view of the operations and provides the language necessary to effectively define problem areas.

A common temptation is for executives to look for a universal management formula that they can apply to their organization. This frame of mind is one the main causes for ineffective management frameworks in staffing. There is no one-size-fits-all framework for all staffing companies. As you will see in this book, there are several variables that must be considered to build an effective management framework, including:

- Well-Defined Growth Strategy
- A Balanced Metrics Portfolio
- Strong Governance Plan.

The Growth Strategy

The first step in building the framework begins with the willingness of the top executive to challenge the current strategy and actively lead the management team in a new direction. That willingness to change must then be followed by a well-defined growth strategy, which is both comprehensive and measurable. With the willingness to change and a strategic direction defined, only then will the executive have the tools to build the right framework to lead their organization.

Many staffing executives are skeptical of the term "strategy." I do have sympathy for this point of view since too often planning sessions are only about defining intent instead of determining ways to make that intent a reality. These types of strategies begin in the conference room and end on a conference call where the new strategy is communicated. Initially, the team may be excited about the growth strategy, but without an effective action plan the new vision fades and within 90 days everyone is back doing the same things they have always done. This failure is usually the most common argument against the effectiveness of strategic planning, when in fact the fault lies with how the strategy was initially created and managed.

> *A well-defined growth strategy contains two key components: targeted financial results and clear objectives for the three staffing performance drivers that lead toward those results.*

Financial objectives must measure top and bottom-line growth, while giving visibility into financial objectives of the strategy. For example, if a staffing organization is going to renew a focus on small and mid-size business to drive up margins, then a measure of that segment's profitability would be appropriate to supplement overall financial measures.

Staffing performance drivers, comprised of a combination of processes and policies, play a critical function within business:

- **The Sales Strategy** establishes the value proposition, the targeted client base, and the sales process necessary to bring the right job orders into the organization.
- **Operational Alignment** drives delivery of those orders, including job order management, sourcing, and submittal management.

- **The Performance-Driven Culture** is strongly influenced by the other two drivers, and also includes an internal hiring process, training, compensation, incentives, and performance management.

These three drivers work together to impact the financial results:

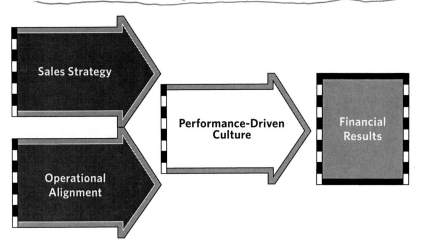

Chapter 3 discusses the sales strategy, operational alignment, and Performance-Driven Culture, while chapter 4 presents the financial impacts of these three drivers.

The executive who has an objective-driven strategy in all areas has taken the first step in defining the management framework. A management team with clear objectives collaborates more effectively, can manage both short and long-term improvements, and has a consistent vision to communicate to its employees. The measurability of objectives also provides important insight into the effectiveness of the strategic improvements, and defines areas of accountability for the management team.

The concept of an objective driven strategy is heavily influenced by the work of Dr. Robert S. Kaplan and Dr. David P. Norton. To learn more about their approach to strategy and management read *The Strategy-Focused Organization: How Balanced Scorecard Companies Thrive in the New Business Environment* and *The Execution Premium: Linking Strategy to Operations for Competitive Advantage.*

The Metrics Portfolio

After the objective of each driver is defined, the next step in building an effective management framework is the metrics portfolio. The need for the right type and amount of metrics is an important consideration. Companies have a tendency to have far too many metrics or far too few. The problem with too many metrics is that the metrics can confuse even the most experienced manager and become so unwieldy that managers stop using them altogether. The problem with too few metrics creates setbacks: if a manager is not measuring enough metrics, then the picture of what is happening in the operation is incomplete.

The quality of metrics is also a common problem. Choose the wrong metrics and you can have significant blind spots. For example, if I have "diversifying my client base" as a client objective, then I know I must increase meeting activity. If I just measure meeting activity with no regard to where the meetings occur, I could just be encouraging my sales team to meet with the same people over and over again. While my meeting numbers have increased, I have done nothing to drive my progress with client diversification on closed sales. Metrics need to be aligned with each driver's objectives and be well defined in order to be effective.

Proper balance is critical. Too often metric systems focus on one driver, while not recording any measurements on the other two. A company may be very strong at metrics around operational alignment. They know their job order coverage rates, quality ratios, and activity trends. However-er, they do not measure sales or individual performance metrics. In this case the organization may be very effective at delivery, but over time the organization will hold on to poor producers for too long and their account base will dwindle. Managers must understand that if they do not measure a behavior, they cannot manage to it. If they cannot manage to it, then the team will begin to believe it is not important and the behavior will suffer. A balanced portfolio that measures objectives around results, sales strategy, operational alignment, and individual performance will give management the visibility it needs to quickly identify problems across the operation.

The Governance Plan

Having a well-defined measurable growth strategy will not impact the organization if the management team does not change its behavior to drive results. Management's job is to drive the right improvements through all levels of the organization. This is done in a multitude of ways, including performance management, process improvement, effective communication, and consistent leadership. The distinct roles managers have in driving continuous improvement in these areas—along with they approach they take to execute these roles—is known as governance.

Effective governance begins with defining the roles of each manager. While that may appear obvious, you would be amazed at the lack of clarity of management roles in organizations. From the executive to the recruiting manager, role clarity is a critical—yet rarely found—component of the overall management framework. Instead, most managers just go with the flow and hope they are doing their jobs properly.

Governance often centers on types of management activities that occur to gain insight on the operations and focus the team in the right direction. Some examples of these activities include formal and informal training, ongoing team motivation, requirements ("req") meetings, sales meetings, performance management meetings, branch meetings, company-wide meetings, and executive team meetings.

Wrapping Up

A management framework based on the performance drivers provides the entire management team clarity of purpose and the data to make the right decisions within the context of the company's overall growth strategy. This additional focus and visibility allows management to drive day-to-day performance, while identifying and implementing strategic operational improvements that breakthrough performance bottlenecks.

The need for this more disciplined approach is accelerated by market forces that continually increase competitive pressures. From more educated buyers to aggressive competitors, strong staffing managers must understand the forces that they face and build the management system and skills required to continually adapt the operations to those challenges.

Chapter 2:
The Competitive Landscape

Clients want more for less. They will often go with the company that provides them the best value with the most current offerings at the appropriate price. To drive growth, companies must take market share from their competitors. The economy is in flux: change is no longer an option, but a critical success factor. Staffing managers must ask the question, "Is my company a passive victim or an active beneficiary of change?"

If managers do not drive competitive improvements, then no one will. Managers are the stewards of the company's future competitiveness, and to ignore that responsibility is to engage in management malpractice. Managers must understand the competitive forces that pressure staffing firms toward a model of continuous improvement. Only then can managers truly understand how to respond effectively.

As a leading authority on company strategy and competeness, Michael Porter offers five competitive forces that have the biggest impact on the future of our industry:[1]

- New Entrants
- Bargaining Power of Buyers
- Power of Suppliers
- Threat of Substitutes
- Rivalry Among Competitors.

These forces work together against your organization as shown in the following graphic.

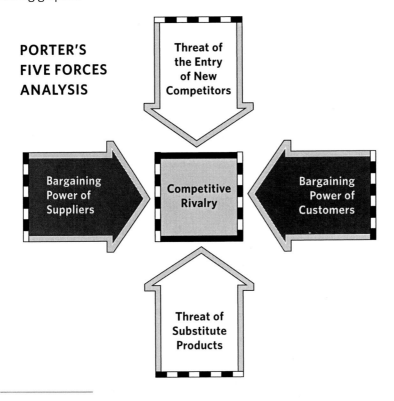

[1] Porter, Michael. "How Competitive Forces Shape Strategy," *Harvard Business Review*, March 3, 2009

Understanding these forces will provide insight on how your company should respond strategically to a rapidly changing marketplace.

New Entrants

"I think I will start a staffing company."

> *One of my neighbors started a company to provide inventory for manufacturers. To start the business he needed to borrow close to $500K, much of which went to lease warehouse space and purchase the necessary inventory. He also needed working capital to give the company the required runway to ramp up sales.*
>
> *Compare this business model with the required cost of starting a staffing company. Most staffing companies can be started with as little as a computer, high speed internet, job boards, and the nominal cost of collateral and a website. And while cash flow remains a significant obstacle to growth, factoring companies and other financial options are available to support the rapidly growing small firm.*

A relatively low barrier to entry is only the beginning. Typical small staffing firms ($10-15M) have distinct advantages over large and mid-size firms when it comes to serving buyers who desire a direct relationship with their vendors. First, many profitable small staffing firms have a sales strategy that focuses on specific technology, geography, industry vertical, or client size, requiring a very simple sales process to execute the strategy. Compare this to larger staffing firms that must sell to companies of various sizes, skill sets, geographies, and must manage multiple sales processes to match the different buying patterns.

Second, small staffing firms encourage a collaborative environment between the sales and recruiting teams. This collaboration allows the recruiting organization to understand and adapt to the clients' needs, thus providing a significant competitive advantage when working directly with hiring managers. This operational alignment significantly simplifies delivery and improves productivity. Large staffing firms that support a variety of client types have to adjust their delivery to fluctuations in volume, response times, skill set, and geographical coverage. This variety demands more complex operational models that tend toward more transactional interaction between the sales and recruiting organizations. While this transactional workflow may be desirable for staffing programs where responsiveness is a competitive differentiator, it can be a significant disadvantage for service-driven clients.

Third, an owner from a small staffing company has significant visibility into client buying trends and can readily assess their operational alignment. This combination of executive authority and visibility acts as the foundations for effective adaptability. In the case of small companies, change is driven by well-informed owners who have the direct knowledge necessary to make the right decisions. In larger staffing firms, distinct management layers—including sales and recruiting managers, operations managers, regional managers and executives—must be combined to provide the same knowledge and authority as one owner from a small firm. This level of complexity in large organizations creates significant obstacles to adaptability.

Executives from mid-size and large staffing firms attempt to bridge the knowledge gap through metrics. Reliance on metrics is a necessary management tool, but it simply cannot provide the same insight as the single executive who is exposed to all elements of the business on a day-to-day basis.

In large firms, authority is also distributed among the different management layers, where the weakest management link determines the effectiveness of the adaptation. In short, for change to be implemented effectively in a large firm, all management must be in agreement, trained, and held accountable for their role in the change. This is a complicated proposition and remains one the greatest challenges for the larger staffing firm.

Why is the staffing industry so fragmented? It is due in large part to the low barriers to entry and the advantages of a small firm in adapting to the ever-changing environment. While economic and regulatory changes may drive consolidation, the wide diversity of staffing firms is a reflection of the diversity of buyers, keeping the niche open for new entrants to establish their foothold in the market.

Bargaining Power of Buyers

"There is plenty of good talent out there."

Several years ago I managed a fairly large staffing operation. Job orders were up while close rates and gross profits remained healthy. Life was good. Then, our largest client called to tell us they were releasing an RFP for the vendor list and things were about to get ugly.

They "invited" us to participate in a reverse online auction. This auction was the brainchild of collaboration between procurement and a consulting group. In this auction, we needed to give them the lowest markup percentage we were willing to accept. As a management team, we decided on our number, and we made an oath not to budge.

The online auction began and all the staffing companies put their proposed markup percentage in the system. It started in the mid-forties, giving us confidence that the number we put in would be competitive. Our confidence lasted about three minutes.

Soon, there were firms who started to bid down to the mid-thirties, then the mid-twenties, and then into the teens. We held firm until we got a private message from the client:

"Your lack of flexibility is endangering your spot on our vendor list."

It took us about 30 seconds to cave.

Subsequently, our gross profit percentage was adjusted by close to 8 points and we lost access to all the direct buyers. We not only lost our competitive advantage, but our profitability took a significant hit. Through centralized procurement, our client was flexing its muscle and this was only a sample of what was to come.

The increasing bargaining power of buyers has been a challenge for staffing firms ever since the beginning of the millennium. The pressure to produce greater ROI has led many buyers to transform their staff augmentation model away from differentiation based on relationships and customer service, and toward a focus on program compliance and performance.

Many firms blame the advent of the Vendor Management Systems (VMS) and their associated programs for this transformation. Actually, VMS is only a symptom of the natural evolution between buyer and vendor as an industry matures. It is only natural for a buyer to drive cost lower, gain visibility into their spending on contract labor, and manage vendors on objective performance measures. This is not unique to the staffing industry. Most buyers will leverage whatever advantages they have to increase the value they get from vendors. The impact cannot be underestimated. Unpredictable job order skill sets, large fluctuations in job order volume, importance of responsiveness, lower productivity ratios, and smaller margins are only some of the operational impacts that staffing firms contend with.

How do these clients continue to retain the upper hand?

Staffing buyers leverage a couple of significant advantages when negotiating with vendors. First, switching vendors is relatively painless. When a company switches vendors, the client loses all institutional knowledge, which could impact service level. Yet this is a mere inconvenience compared to the savings these programs can provide. In the end, it is very difficult for a staffing vendor to become an indispensable partner. It is unfortunate, but in many cases staffing firms are too easily replaced.

Second, many staffing firms become highly dependent on a few large clients. This weakens staffing companies in two ways: The obvious impact is the more dependent a staffing company is on a client, the more the staffing company is willing to reduce rates. Anyone who has experienced a reverse auction understands how desperate staffing firms can become when a large client negotiates for price concessions.

The other impact is more insidious. As staffing companies realize more business from fewer clients, they can lose the ability to land and grow new business. In effect they turn into a delivery-driven organization versus a sales-driven organization. A weakened sales organization increases the dependency on current accounts, thereby weakening a staffing company's negotiating position. Management often does not realize the level of dependency until pressure is applied by existing clients. By then the staffing company is in a weakened position and unable to change as quickly.

Power of Suppliers

"Why pay someone when I can hunt the job boards myself?"

What can weaken the bargaining power of buyers and shift more power to staffing companies? A shift in supply and demand breaks the transactional VMS model. The commoditization of our industry is predicated on readily available talent. Earlier in my career I wrote an article describing how the war for talent may undermine transactional VMS programs because recruiting methods would have to change as the talent becomes less available. To speak of a war for talent today may seem out of place, depending on the space you serve. Nonetheless, the long-term trends, especially in IT graduation and retirement rates, point to talent supply issues in the future.

One can argue that there are already fewer qualified candidates available in some areas than there were before the recent recession, but the increased visibility of talent through social media and job boards has acted as a buffer and has bought buyers more time. Will a decrease in talent supply lead to more opportunity for staffing firms? Much of that depends on the evolution of another competitive force: The Threat of Substitutes.

Threat of Substitutes

"Staffing will eventually transform into payroll services."

The Threat of Substitutes is the danger that alternative services may have on the demand on a particular industry. A good example of the impact a substitute product can have on an industry is the affect MP3 technology had on the CD industry. The demand for CDs reduced dramatically because a substitute product was more cost effective and convenient for the customer. The MP3 caused a fundamental shift in the industry. Whether there is a substitute service for staffing that could have the same impact as the MP3 to the CD industry is uncertain, but options for buyers are increasing and could impact the demand for traditional staffing providers.

The clearest example of the threat of substitutes can be seen from the impact job boards and social networking sites have had on recruiting companies' competitive advantage. I have worked with several organizations whose massive candidate database was their key differentiator. Years ago, this was true: If you had millions of candidates in your database then you had something very few competitors had.

Today, even the smallest startup has access to massive databases. The differentiator is no longer having access to those candidates; instead, how quickly and effectively you source and place those candidates creates the difference. Often, massive candidate databases are so poorly configured that they actually become a hindrance to productivity, forcing recruiters to vet through hundreds of marginally qualified resumes before identifying a qualified candidate.

Another threat from substitution resides in the continued evolution of the outsourcing model. Outsourcing, whether it is offshore or onshore, has always been a threat to staffing. This threat looms large in the IT space with cloud computing presenting a potential large-scale threat. While the outsourcing segment seems to always be in a state of flux, the advent and adoption of cloud computing could be exceptionally disruptive to the IT services market. Cloud as a disruptive change agent may increase demand in the short-term, but it also may prove to be a significant long-term threat to the staffing industry.

Rivalry

"Can I find services cheaper overseas? Can they work 24x7?"

Anyone who has more than five years of experience in the staffing industry knows the intensity of pricing pressures. While VMS plays a significant role in driving pricing down, the competitive landscape encourages it to happen. As long as there are competitors who are willing to do the work for less and there is a low barrier to entry, pricing pressures will continue. Some firms have embraced this dynamic by increasing operational bandwidth through processes and automation built for speed and volume, while at the same time limiting fixed sales and recruiting costs. In short, a firm's ability to respond quickly and cheaply is a competitive advantage.

The pinnacle of this model may be in offshoring, where low-cost, educated labor works 24x7 to submit candidates at a rate that domestic recruiters have difficulty matching. Quality may be an issue, but more companies make offshoring their primary delivery model. The increasing maturity of the offshore model will likely raise the quality of candidates recruited offshore, thus reducing the competitive advantage of domestic recruiting. This is especially true of large, national accounts where responsiveness and volume are key competitive differentiators. To avoid the inevitable commoditization of the transactional staffing model, many firms attempt to move up the value chain by offering additional services. As staffing companies sensed a changing marketplace, many of them developed offerings around workforce management, specific technologies, or industry vertical. These approaches are becoming increasingly prevalent regardless of the size of firm.

These competitive forces should not discourage managers; rather, it should provide important context on how to manage and lead their teams. First, managers must understand that the market is constantly shifting.

Second, they must respond to the ongoing shifts by building an adaptable firm. Finally, staffing managers must embrace these competitive forces and lead the change that will ensure short-term success and survival long-term.

Wrapping Up

You now have insight into the most powerful competitive forces at work against a staffing company. Regardless of how it may sound, the pressures on the staffing industry are really no greater than you would find in any industry that continues to mature. On a positive note, the ability to acquire just-in-time specialized talent is not going away; if anything, it is going to increase in importance.

Chapter 3:
Internal Ammunition—
Strategic Drivers

Now that we have discussed the general competitive landscape within the staffing industry, we can move to the core drivers within a particular staffing organization that contribute to its competitive advantage, and ultimately drive financial results.

Strategic drivers are the specific areas within a staffing organization that contribute to its competitive advantage and drive financial results. To quickly recap part of Chapter 1, a staffing company has three drivers:

- Sales Strategy
- Operational Alignment
- Performance-Driven Culture.

These drivers can be attributed consistently to all staffing organizations. However, implementation of them varies from company to company.

Thus, implementation creates unique competitive differentiators.

In staffing, the sales strategy heavily influences the other two strategic drivers, because it is the sales strategy that acts as the voice of the customer as well as the company's competitive position in the national or global marketplace. To learn more about the definition of the sales strategy, I encourage you to read *Building a Winning Sales Force* by Andris A. Zoltners, Prabhakant Sinha, and Salley E. Lorimer.

Operational alignment reflects how efficient your processes are at delivering services to the client. An operationally efficient company has a well-aligned sales and recruiting organization along with processes and tools that enable the teams to compete with other staffing firms. To remain operationally competitive requires continuous improvement and awareness of changes within the client base as well as changes in the market as a whole. Areas of focus in operational alignment are job order management, sourcing, submittal management, and assignment management.

The Performance-Driven Culture captures how an effective team is built, managed, and developed. Staffing is a people business and can make up for significant deficiencies within the sales strategy and operations. An unhealthy culture, on the other hand, may undermine an otherwise well-managed organization. Because of that possibility, culture is one of the most difficult drivers to correct. Performance-Driven Culture includes hiring, performance management, team building, compensation, policy development, as well as compensation and other types of incentives.

Part 1: The Sales Strategy

Sitting across the table from a certain staffing executive, I could not help but be impressed. He was obviously intelligent, had a strong passion for the business, and was charismatic. He had built his company to close to $15 million, but he was the only rainmaker and he failed time after time to grow an effective sales force.

When I asked him why he was failing, he began to lament the lack of talent and work ethic in the marketplace. Experienced sales people were either stubborn or complacent and people with no experience were simply too much work to develop.

What was more revealing were the three questions he could not answer, including:

- *Why do clients choose you over the competition?*
- *What types of clients are you targeting?*
- *How do you manage your sales people?*

All I got was a blank stare. The simple truth is that talented executives close business by their unique talents – they are A players. But the executives who have the skills to make B players successful are the ones that build a productive sales team. They provide the structure to drive behavior and the coaching to build expertise.

Effective executives and managers understand one simple fact: Staffing is a sales-driven business. Even with the operational challenges that companies face today, a well-executed sales strategy still should garner the most attention from all levels of staffing management.

This attention is well-warranted, because it is the sales strategy that determines the future growth of the business and provides the flexibility needed to adjust to the changing whims of the current client base. Your sales strategy defines your target accounts, what services you provide, and the sales process you use to take it to market. An organization that does not have a sales strategy aligned with their sales culture lacks the ability to coordinate resources consistently, communicate value to the market, establish appropriate client relationships, and ensure effective delivery of solutions. A staffing company without an effectively defined and managed sales strategy is whistling past the graveyard.

The sales strategy is divided into three separate parts: the value proposition you take to market, buyers that you pursue, and the sales process that helps ensure the long-term financial health of the organization.

THE VALUE PROPOSITION

Staffing is a relationship business, but are there other reasons why clients should buy from you? What makes your company unique? The value proposition is the foundation of your company's narrative to the marketplace. It is composed of compelling reasons why buyers should choose you over the competition.

When I joined the staffing industry, most value propositions focused on the ability of the account manager to build a strong, trusting relationship with the client. I have seen sales people establish strong relationships in a variety of ways. Some rely on their experience and knowledge of the industry to build immediate credibility, while others will connect on more personal level through things such as shared interest in a charity, professional organization, or even sports teams. Those who think that sports are an inadequate way to connect to a buyer need to come to the South, where college football is one of the most frequent topics of passionate conversation. These types of relationships are built primarily on likability and strong customer service. Those elements still play a strong role in many staffing firms today. However, as the industry responded to the competitive forces outlined in Chapter 2, many staffing companies have added different value propositions to compel clients to buy their services:

- Speed, Price and Scale
- Specialization
- Customer Service
- Workforce Management Solutions (WMS)

Speed, Price, and Scale: People complain about the quality this model provides, but it is hard to argue that there is not a place for a highly transactional staffing model within all staffing sectors. Even in the IT sector, most Fortune 500 companies have been willing to forego candidate quality and customer service for organizations that can deliver a lot of candidates quickly and at a low price point across its entire enterprise. This model is enabled by online resume databases and job boards that focus on readily available talent. For the time being, the differentiation of the proprietary database has been weakened by the increased visibility of the candidate pool via online tools. Note: The database may see its differentiation rise again if the readily available talent pool substantially declines.

In the present time, online candidate databases have also enabled the offshoring model as well. While offshoring efforts initially focused on sourcing candidates, there are several staffing companies that leverage offshore resources for the entire recruiting lifecycle even for high-level skill sets. The sustainability of this model is yet to be determined. Nonetheless, it is a trend worth noting. The offshoring model represents a significant cost savings to recruiting companies.

Specialization: Specialization is another value proposition common in the professional staffing arena. It is often seen as a way to gain access to different buyers while alleviating gross profit pressures that have increased over the last decade. Choosing a niche specialization may encompass delivery ownership or just the promise of a higher-qualified candidate through more effective sourcing and qualification.

The most common types of specialization include specific technologies or industry verticals. Specialization aligns well with difficult-to-find skill sets and/or high-level professionals that are difficult to source, qualify, and close. Temporary doctors (locum tenens) are a great example of this type of specialization.

This strategy can struggle with top-line growth, but if delivered properly, it can leverage core operational capabilities to move up the value chain and drive up profitability.

Customer Service: Customer service is the traditional differentiator for staffing firms that rely on local branches to service their accounts with dedicated personnel. Customers benefit from a local team that understands the local environment, quickly responds to conflicts, and maintains close relationships with key buyers.

With many large companies centralizing their procurement of talent and closely managing their rules of engagement, the branch model experiences significant stress. The question of whether the branch can effectively support limited access accounts is an appropriate one because their cost per submittal is typically much higher than a centralized recruiting team. In addition, a branch model built on customer service struggles to compete when speed and volume are the competitive differentiators.

Branches tend to thrive when they have an aggressive prospecting strategy that continually identifies and lands new buyers who desire customer service and quality delivery. These buyers can be found by focusing on mid-market accounts or by finding a way to work around the rules of engagement to achieve a competitive advantage.

Workforce Management Solutions (WMS): Several staffing companies have expanded their services to feature aspects of Workforce Management Solutions (WMS), including payroll services, risk management, and managed services. All of these provide value to the client by reducing the cost and risk of contingent labor. Both the payroll and managed services (as defined by outsourced management of the client's staffing program) drive commoditization of the staffing industry. Cases exist in which the Managed Services Provider (MSP) is a staffing provider. This combination of services highlights the potential synergies between staffing and WMS. While most companies who provide both staffing and WMS keep operations separate, the insights and relationships provided through WMS offer a competitive edge to the staffing organization.

For some companies, marketing a unique value proposition proves to be a slippery slope. As competitive forces have made staffing a commodity to many clients, the industry has tried to respond by moving up the value chain. One approach staffing companies take is positioning themselves as professional services organizations.

This is especially common in the IT staffing vertical. When salespeople tell me that their companies specialize in Quality Assurance projects, I always ask myself if this is marketing fluff. It only takes a few questions on how projects are staffed and managed to see clearly if this expertise is real, or part imaginative spin and part wishful thinking.

Marketing is best when it is based on true capabilities. Trying to market something you are not built to deliver is a risk you might be willing to take, but just keep in mind that reputation and trust is the foundation of our service.

Understanding the value proposition is critical for managers. It determines how you market, how you deliver, and how you identify your target clientele.

Matching the value proposition to the right buyers is a key success factor to increasing efficiency and driving growth. This leads us to the second element of the sales strategy of targeting buyers.

TARGETED BUYERS

Talk to any sales manager and you will hear that most sales people struggle to qualify accounts. We hire sales people because they see potential in every opportunity, but the flip side of that equation is that sales people also bring in business that the company is not built to support. As a manager, your challenge is to motivate your sales force to pursue the accounts which best fit your business.

The amount of work necessary to prepare for and schedule the first meeting is significant, and a sales person may or may not be enthusiastic about the prospect. If a staffing manager has to requalify an account – especially one that the sales person has worked hard to win – and then inform the sales person that their business cannot support the new client, then it is demoralizing for the sales person. By developing a clear definition of what accounts should be targeted, the staffing manager can help ensure the right accounts get the focus they deserve.

The following graphic captures how targeting staffing buyers traditionally progresses through the sales process. First, you begin with a list of target accounts that meet you criteria. Second, you identify the program stakeholders who will approve you as a vendor. Third, learn to maneuver through the rules of engagement to eventually develop a relationship with the hiring manager. This diagram is not meant to be universally accurate, but shows the different elements that may be involved in targeting accounts.

Target Accounts

The targeting phase organizes sales activity around accounts that find the value proposition compelling and have the right characteristics to make a profitable client. In many ways staffing managers can choose to segment and prioritize their accounts including:

- Company size
- Geography
- Industry vertical
- Number of contractors
- Bill rates or markup percentage
- Rules of engagement
- Level of risk
- Hiring activity.

Anyone who has managed a sales team understands the need for a basic structure for the sales activity. Targeting accounts is the most fundamental structure a manager can provide; moreover, targeting plays a critical role in ensuring a more productive sales desk.

Program Managers

After determining the company target list, the next step is to develop the selling approach to individual buyers and/or stakeholders of the staffing program. Most companies require that staffing companies are included on an approved vendor list. These programs often are managed internally by Human Resources or Procurement. They may also be managed externally by an MSP. These stakeholders play a significant role in deciding who can provide staffing services, the rules of engagement with the hiring manager, and the ongoing management of the program.

Some programs are highly regulated and seek to minimize or eliminate communication between the staffing firm and the hiring manager. The elimination of this interaction creates a level playing field for all the vendors, and saves hiring managers from constant hounding by staffing firms seeking to gain competitive advantage. Other programs allow approved vendors limited access to managers based on whether a manager has active job orders or submittals. Yet other programs manage some logistics of the staffing program, but carry very little authority in managing the relationship between the staffing firm and the hiring manager.

Regardless of how highly regulated a program is, selling directly to the hiring manager remains a key success factor for many sales strategies. Working directly with hiring managers leads to better requirements gathering and allows the staffing firm to develop strong relationships with the direct decision makers. These differentiators reap significant competitive advantage. For this reason, many staffing firms hold access to the hiring manager as a prerequisite to pursue business. Those companies choose only to participate in programs that allow access to, or intentionally work around, hiring manager contact restrictions. Highly regulated recruiting/placement programs are here to stay. So how do you decide which programs to pursue?

Rules of Engagement

Staffing companies need to be aware of the common misstep of ineffectively vetting the programs they decide to pursue. In essence, the approach these companies take is that "any client is a good client." However, buyers manage their programs differently, and if a company chooses to pursue an account that does not align well with their delivery model, then they could be doing their organization more harm than good. This is especially true for small and mid-sized firms whose delivery model is more limited.

Our family has a 12 lb. Bijon Havanese named Lucy who insists on chasing after any car she possibly can. I am always amazed that she sees no danger in running next to the spinning wheels of a 5,000 pound minivan. Her determination, while admirable, is badly misplaced, and begs for a significant Darwinian correction.

While I have yet to see sales executives chase after anything potentially life threatening, I have seen them pursue and land accounts that can break the back of an entire staffing operation. For future reference, beware the Fortune 500 account with a sexy name, high volume, low margins, and lots of vendors – unless your company is built to support the business.

I worked with a company that was a branch-centric, quality-focused staffing firm that landed such an account after many years of pursuing procurement. The day the account was landed brought a lot of excitement to the team. This was an account that anyone at a cocktail party would love to brag about.

What were not impressive were the margins and the productivity of the account. After months of support and hundreds of submittals, not only was the submittal-to-hire ratio one of the highest in the company, but they had to make three placements there to equal one placement at their mid-market accounts. They had taxed their operations to the limit to support an account that was not willing to pay them for the effort.

So before judging Lucy's poor decision making to chase large vehicles, you may want to ask yourself if you are pursuing accounts that are similarly dangerous to your staffing operations – and, if so, what is driving that decision.

Qualifying accounts is easy to ignore because often it is very difficult to know whether the account is a good fit until you begin the working relationship. Be mindful that ineffective targeting of staffing programs carries significant costs to a company's bottom line and reputation. Not only do poorly targeted accounts waste sales resources, they can break the recruiting model and undermine a company's reputation.

The decision to pursue highly regulated programs poses competitive challenges for new vendors, because incumbent vendors may work around the rules of engagement. Hiring managers frequently will ignore the staffing programs rules of engagement to work directly with incumbent vendors. In addition, gatekeepers who have the flexibility in how the program is managed may favor one company over another. This is prevalent enough that it is safe to assume that any program with strong rules of engagement is enforced inconsistently. This inconsistent enforcement creates a significant competitive advantage for incumbent vendors.

Hiring Managers

Once you have targeted the right accounts and the right programs, the next level for targeting is the hiring manager. Direct access to the hiring manager remains the holy grail of selling within the staffing industry. Working directly with the managers can lower submittal-to-hire ratios and generate healthier gross profits. It is important to understand that not all managers are created equal. Some require more attention than others. How does a company effectively focus its sales team to identify managers who will eventually buy from them, and ideally bring them years of profitable business? The following decision criteria can help:

- Hiring authority
- Perception of service

Hiring Authority: The hiring authority is a manager's ability to influence the process of hiring talent from agencies. This is not an issue in less-regulated staffing programs. However, in highly-regulated programs, hiring managers do not necessarily control the budget. Instead, the staffing program has final approval to release funds and approve the placement. Many managers respond to this situation by developing ways to circumvent the program in order to procure the talent in the way that best meets their needs. I refer to this this circumvention as "Rogue Spend."

Pursuing Rogue Spend can be very profitable and provides significant competitive advantages. It requires strong relationships with buyers who believe it is in their best interest to break the rules and have the fortitude to withstand the political pressure that comes with circumventing the program. It also is important to keep in mind that there are risks to the staffing company because actively working with managers who choose not to cooperate with the program can cause distrust between you and the gatekeeper. How aggressively you decide to pursue Rogue Spend should be influenced by the long-term account strategy, the strength of your relationships with the program managers, and the ability to craft trusting relationships with hiring managers.

Another common workaround is the use of Statement of Work (SOW) procedures. As the name suggests, the SOW typically requires some type of deliverable associated with the work, which suggests that staffing companies are not equipped to respond. That said, frequently managers leverage SOWs either to avoid the processes of an existing program or to simplify the hiring of multiple resources for a project. In those cases, the staffing company and hiring manager may craft the SOW based on time and materials with very few, if any, deliverables. Being able to purchase services through a SOW provides the manager much more control over the process of acquiring talent, and allows the manager to develop a level of partnership with staffing firms that may be impossible to achieve through the staffing program.

Business unit spend is also a common way to find business outside of the program. This spend commonly is found within the business units that may not fall under the authority of the staffing program. Whether it is the CFO responding to changing compliance requirements or a VP of Marketing looking for a better Customer Relationship Management system (CRM), these executives may have the budget authority needed to make decisions outside of the staffing program.

Perception of Service: Another important qualification of the direct buyer is to understand how direct buyers perceive staffing on the value chain. This perception influences what they are willing to pay as well as service-level expectations. Even with strong trends of commoditization oc-curring within all areas of staffing, do not assume all managers think alike. Understanding how managers and other buyers perceive the value of staff-ing can play a critical role in establishing a long and mutually profitable relationship.

An effective way of assessing how a buyer perceives staffing is to look at it from the perspective of the value the buyer expects to receive along with the price point the buyer is willing to pay. The following buyer matrix

	TRADITIONAL STAFFING	VALUE-ADDED STAFFING
HIGH PRICE POINT	Service-driven buyer, who values relationships with staffing vendors and the service they provide. Willing to pay above market rates to work with firms they trust.	Value-added buyers who desire and are willing to pay for a level of specialization among staffing providers. High expectations on quality, but are willing to pay for it.
LOW PRICE POINT	Buyer who views staffing as a commodity and will only engage staffing firms in a transactional way. Typically these managers advocate highly regulated staffing programs.	Buyers who have a disconnect between what they have paid for versus the service they receive. Willing to pay low market rates, but expect value added service.

captures different ways buyers may perceive staffing.

Low Price Point/Traditional Staffing: These buyers view all staffing firms the same. Therefore, they do not see any value in developing relationships with specific firms and/or their sales people. They embrace highly regulated programs that provide a barrier between them and the staffing firm.

High Price Point/Traditional Staffing: They value the service that staffing provides and believe paying more will give them access to better candidates and service level from the firms. These buyers are willing to view staffing providers as partners and are the most likely to find ways around a highly regulated program either by working around program rules or leveraging SOWs to procure their talent.

Low Price Point/Value-Added: These buyers can pose some of the most difficult challenges for staffing providers. Sales people must develop relationships with these buyers and provide a high level of service, but are unable to charge for that time and expertise. These buyers can have an inflated view of the value a consultant brings to an assignment, causing ongoing maintenance issues that can take away from new, more profitable business. Unless a sales person is able to quickly build significant volume with this type of manager, it may be best to avoid this type of business.

High Price Point/Value-Added: These buyers expect best-in-class talent and will pay a premium to obtain it. To ensure a high service level, they look for specific expertise from their staffing organizations. These are the targeted buyers for staffing firms who wish to blur the line between staffing and consulting services by specializing in a niche technology or industry vertical. For these buyers, specialization drives the quality and consistency they need.

It is important to recognize that as with any model, attempts to categorize human behavior will overgeneralize. Nonetheless, understanding how hiring managers perceive staffing is an important step in qualifying how much time you should spend with a prospect, and how to best express value in a way that they would find compelling.

Selling directly to the hiring manager is the desirable approach for most staffing firms. To sell effectively one must show creativity, persistence, and focus. For this reason, more companies are formalizing and investing in their sales processes to enable their sales teams to maneuver through an increasingly competitive environment.

Golf remains one of the best avenues to get to know clients, especially in a relationship-driven industry such as staffing. So when I was asked to play with a senior VP of the largest telecom provider in the country, I saw a great opportunity to establish an important relationship and spend time educating the client on our company.

I was playing one of my best games in years. After the first few holes, it became clear that I had a lot in common with the VP. We were getting along great, and while I was trying to find a way to discuss business, he torpedoed my plan when he looked me in the eye and said: "You might think you are different, but all staffing firms are basically the same."

I quickly realized that our successful history at the account, the low submittal-to-hire ratios, strong coverage rates, and number of placements would not matter to him. He viewed staffing as a commodity.

When I thought more about it, I realized the highly structured staffing program was built to turn staffing into a commodity. All providers were the same, but that was because his company gave no avenue for high-quality firms to differentiate themselves. There are two lessons I learned from this brief conversation:

- *Regardless of the company you build, client perception is paramount.*
- *If your client base views you as a commodity, that is what you will become.*

THE SALES PROCESS

How you sell – or your sales process – represents the set of activities that your sales organization must master to leverage the company's value proposition to the target buyers. How the sales process is defined varies per company based on strategy, team composition, the nature of the value proposition and other factors. Successful companies have been able to define an effective sales process and align it with how they hire, train, and manage their sales people. Without the effective linkage from process to behavior, a sales process is nothing but theory, bringing little or no value to the organization.

In the following figure, you will see a sample sales process that provides the outline for the rest of this section. These steps should act as a starting point for defining your team's sales process.

The cyclical sales process focuses on the sales person's activities required to grow the business. This process begins with effective targeting of prospects and ends with successfully maintaining and growing current clients.

Lead Management

What is more central to sales than the effective generation and management of leads? When you ask people what defines a lead, you will get several different answers. Some sales people use the term "lead" to mean a person, a company, or a specific opportunity. Well, that is fine if you do not see value in managing lead generation. However, this lack of definition of a lead can cause confusion among your team and make it more difficult to measure and to manage lead generation activities. This confusion is often caused by important differences between leads as entities (companies and managers), as market intelligence (mergers, new projects, etc.), and as distinct opportunities. Each one of those can be considered some type of lead. Because the actions to follow up effectively on them differ radically, we must discuss them as unique items.

Companies and Managers: Manager and company names are important. You need to capture and follow-up on these key individuals. The purpose of these leads is to determine to whom you need to sell, and who belongs in your account funnel and account planning process.

Market Intelligence: The same can be said for market intelligence. As an example, you may find out that the company is expanding or is going through a merger. This is strategic information that is used to further relationships and improve the overall approach to the account. While this information is important, you may not need to act on it urgently. Still, you need to manage it through a more deliberate process to take full advantage of the situation.

Distinct Opportunities: Opportunities are about the here and now, so they require immediate action. A distinct opportunity is defined by an urgent hiring need with a qualified company and a specific hiring manager. Opportunities represent leads that are closest to the dollar and must be acted on quickly. Unlike names and market intelligence, opportunities that are not acted on immediately disappear, and the opportunity is lost.

By defining these leads separately, the staffing manager sets specific expectations of behavior and manages to those expectations. Company names need to be added to the funnel target list, while opportunities need immediate follow-up along with a candidate to proactively sell. Clearly defined activities for distinct lead types enables more effective use of information, thus ensuring the sales team is focused on the right activities.

Establish Trust/Credibility

After leads are converted into meetings, the account manager must build trust and credibility. Trust is elusive, yet it is one of most critical components for why people buy. Buyers must trust that what they purchase provides the expected value. Trust does play a different role based on what the buyer purchases and how that purchase provides value. For example, when it comes to purchasing simple commodities, value is often tangible and easy to measure. Necessary? If I go to a grocery store to buy an apple, I trust that the apple is going to be free of worms. If I find worms, other than the emotional distress, how have I really been impacted? The cost of the apple is nominal. I can show the store the worms and get a refund. Sure, it is possible that the store may deny responsibility, but now I know I need to take my business elsewhere and all I have lost is 79 cents.

Business-to-business selling is not simple. The ROI of many products and services are not immediate and can be very difficult to measure objectively. It is simply impossible for the buyer to know the return on what they buy. To make matters even more complex, larger purchases require a long-term relationship with the buyer. One cannot simply go down the street to another grocery store. The inability to understand immediately the return, and the difficulty of deconstructing large purchases, elevates the role of trust in the buying decision.

It is the sales person's job to make the leap of faith palatable to the buyer by building a trusting relationship. The subtlety of how you build that trust differs from buyer to buyer, based on how they are measured and their roles within the organizations. The type of trust varies greatly when dealing with a procurement officer than when working with a direct buyer.

Qualify Opportunity

"A good hockey player plays where the puck is. A great hockey player plays where the puck is going to be. " —*Wayne Gretzky*

In addition to lead management and building trust, a sales organization must do everything it can to get in front of qualified opportunities before they hit the marketplace. While any sales person can find one or two job orders, one of the biggest barriers to effective time management is not organizing tasks but ensuring that sales people prioritize their time where there is the most opportunity for contract spend. As anyone with industry experience knows, there tends to be large pockets of contract spend in different areas depending on the nature of projects that are occurring. It is the sales person's job to get in front of those projects to give their company a competitive advantage. Every project has a life of its own and has different factors that impact how those needs are eventually filled. A sales process should provide structure and discipline to verify the scope and success factors of any given opportunity, and prioritize the sales person's efforts accordingly.

When qualifying project driven opportunities, the sales person should consider three distinct elements: budget, urgency, and scope (BUS for short).

Qualification Question 1: Is the Budget Approved?

Understanding how positions are funded and where they occur in the funding process is an important part of qualifying opportunities. For companies that run all contingent labor spend through a staffing program, understanding the state of the funding is based on knowing the program's process for approving funds. A significant part of a program's purpose is to provide the processes necessary to approve funding jobs before they are released to vendors.

Projects that are funded outside of a formal staffing program can turn out to be a wild goose chase for the account manager if they do not verify the source of the funding. In some cases the hiring managers have an approved departmental budget, while others receive funding from the business units they are supporting. Sales people who understand how projects are funded will ask the right questions to ensure that the hiring managers have approved funding to hire contingent labor. Sales people who choose not to qualify funding are risking working with a manager who may overestimate their authority. This is especially true for managers who say they can work around a staffing program. These managers only discover their limitations when they are prepared to make an offer and need to generate the purchase order. Only when the purchase order is denied and the manager is forced to restart the hiring process do managers understand the teeth of the program's enforcement.

Similar concerns also may be found when working with managers in companies that have no formalized staffing program. Whether it is through a different funding vehicle such as a SOW or just ordinary staffing, verifying that funding for projects is approved is a critical step in the qualification process.

Qualification Question 2: Is it Urgent?

To determine a project's urgency, you must understand its business impact and the ramifications if it is not completed on time. Staffing firms work on filling positions that become available for a variety of reasons. Positions that are filled quickly are the ones that have real consequences for the hiring manager and the company as a whole. But not all positions are crucial. Occasions arise when managers are uncertain if they need to hire. They have received approval to hire, so they go through the motions of the hiring process. While this scenario is more common with direct hire positions, it is also seen in contingent staffing, especially when there is un-certainty in the scope and/or timelines of projects. In these situations, the managers tend to drag out the hiring process using the excuse of trying to find the "perfect" candidates. This reluctance to pull the trigger can extend the hiring process over weeks or months. For the hiring manager, the risk of hiring is greater than the risk of not hiring. "Decision paralysis" sets in and no decision is made. The positions remain vacant.

Compare that to a manager running a critical project who has a strict deadline to make, or has customers pressuring him to provide better ser-vice. Those managers understand that they cannot afford to wait for the perfect candidate; instead, they have to make do with an imperfect but sat-isfactory candidate. In these cases, the manager looks for ways to screen the candidate into the job, while understanding that there may be some learning curve or changes to the job description to meet the qualifications of the candidate.

Many people would look at the second manager and say that this man-ager is making a compromise that could haunt him later. It is the second manager who has the more realistic view of what it means to hire a new employee. There is no such thing as a perfect candidate. A manager who searches for the perfect candidate to hire is either inexperienced or has no urgent need to fill the position.

Qualification Question 3: Is the Scope Well Defined?

Most hiring managers are busy. That is why they are hiring. Situations arise in which managers know they need help, but they cannot define exactly what type of help they need, much less be able to match their needs to what is available in the marketplace. Asking the right questions about overall team size, the number of contract positions, experience levels needed, technical skills, and cultural fit usually is enough to confirm the manager knows the scope of contingent labor that he needs. Less experienced managers often struggle to define the talent requirements of the project as well as how to manage the hiring of multiple contractors. If the sales person finds themselves working with this type of hiring manager, it presents an excellent opportunity to provide value-added advice and services that could lead to exclusive business for the staffing company.

A manager with poorly defined talent requirements and project scope can frustrate you. They often ask you to re-recruit on changing requirements, have inadequate on-boarding procedures, and have poorly organized workloads leading to team turnover. This becomes a next to impossible situation when the requirements are managed through a highly regulated program where getting specific feedback on the hiring process can be challenging.

Qualifying the project opportunities is just one level of this process that a sales person must manage. Once they know they are selling to the right areas of the client, they also need to qualify each job order before it enters the delivery organization. The details of job order qualification are addressed in the Operational Alignment section.

Present and Close Solution

Finding leads, building trust, and qualifying opportunities is simply not enough if the jobs cannot be presented and closed effectively. Whether it is for a team of individuals or for a single resource, how a staffing company responds to an opportunity needs to be defined by the manner in which the client makes the buying decision. That sounds obvious. In theory, it is obvious. Nonetheless, it is interesting to see how companies present their solutions without taking into account what the client views as important. Is it speed? Is it price? Is it a fully vetted candidate? Following are examples of what some managers expect and how those expectations should impact the presentation of the solution.

Speed: You know things are bad when your candidate's chance of getting a job depends on how deep they are in a pile of resumes. There are staffing programs whose main objective is to get resumes out quickly and turn off the spigot. Then employees of the program or the hiring manager sift through the submittals to determine if there are any candidates who may be qualified for the job. They search for candidates who are good enough to do the job while having very little concern for finding the best candidates. In those cases, speed is of the utmost importance and not the quality of the candidate.

It is important for a staffing company to recognize if what the company delivers is responsive enough. Companies that struggle with responsiveness must either streamline delivery or change the sales strategy to identify buyers who better match the company's delivery process.

Price or Value: As mentioned earlier, I was in a reverse auction for a large, Fortune 500 firm that was asking staffing vendors to give them their best markup for their services. Initially, I was thinking that it would go no lower than 25%, because anything lower would be borderline insanity. I watched in horror as the low bid went all the way down to 12%. What I witnessed were companies that either did not understand their financial models or ones that were going to lie about what they were paying their employees. Either way, I learned never to underestimate what competitors are willing to do to earn business.

Understanding price sensitivity is critical when presenting solutions or even when deciding to do business in the first place. It is easy to try to become more competitive by lowering your price instead of selling on value. Value speaks directly to solving the problems the client faces and being able to communicate why your approach best solves those problems. There are managers who look for value, but are cynical that a staffing firm can be anything more than a commodity. By figuring out a way to provide unexpected value, a company can elevate itself above the competition and have their proposals taken more seriously by hiring managers.

Some examples of value-add that hiring managers may find compelling are:

- Consultative requirements gathering
- Recruiting process focusing on passive, best-in-class candidates
- In-person or video screenings
- Customized executive summaries tailored to the job
- Skill testing
- Reference checks (Clients who demand speed think they pay for and get this service, but they do not).

These activities all cost money to provide, so it is important to understand what is valuable to each specific buyer. Unfortunately, staffing companies commonly add services believing that the manager should find them valuable, only to learn that managers do not find them valuable. The only thing added is cost.

To afford the value-added approach to staffing, there must be a return in either margin, productivity, or both. To clarify, either the client is willing to pay more for the additional service, or they generate a volume of business in a productive way with higher job order close rates and lower submittal-to-hire ratios.

Deliver Solution

After the candidate is hired, the service to the buyer does not end. Typically, delivery is viewed from an administrative standpoint. This includes how contractors are on-boarded and managed as well as how effectively the client is invoiced. However, a comprehensive sales process must take into account everything that impacts the client experience and ensure that service levels are maintained. Too often the front office is highly customer-focused, but that focus is lost after the placement is made. A drop in service level undermines client confidence which can then lead to a client going elsewhere for their staffing needs.

There are many different ways a staffing company can address these potential delivery issues including:

- Accountability of sales personnel to provide the right billing information.
- Secondary review of information to ensure that recruiting provides the correct pay information.
- Formal orientation for new contractors to ensure accurate tax and benefit information is entered.
- Systematic follow-up with the clients and contractors to head off any potential issues.
- Periodic follow-up by management with clients to ensure service levels are maintained.

Regardless of how well assignments are delivered, issues will arise. Properly addressing issues presents an opportunity for staffing companies to differentiate themselves through effective conflict management.

Even minor issues may transform quickly into significant conflicts that threaten the relationship between the client and the staffing company. To prevent a crisis from occurring, it is critical that problems do not fester and staffing managers are kept informed of conflicts/issues that are impacting the client. This openness can be a lot to ask of the sales team, who may be threatened by telling their manager about issues on their client site. The staffing manager has the responsibility to create an environment that encourages open communication by removing the threat of serious reprisal if issues are communicated.

In the end, the staffing manager is the point of escalation when serious issues arise. This escalation to the staffing manager shows the firm's commitment in addressing any issues as well as allowing for financial remediation if necessary. Staffing managers must use discernment in determining when they should and should not get directly involved. The reasons for this are threefold:

- Addressing issues allows sales people to develop their craft.
- By allowing sales people to address issues themselves, they can increase their credibility with the client.
- Involving themselves prematurely, staffing managers trivialize their authority and potentially impact their ability to address larger issues at a later date.

Maintain and Grow

One of the biggest frustrations of staffing managers is how to ensure that sales people are doing what is necessary to increase penetration at their existing accounts. It is very common for a sales person to develop relationships with only a small portion of a client company and be successful. While that success may work for that individual, it does not position the company for long-term growth. Maintaining and growing accounts requires continually increasing your knowledge about the client's business and developing new key relationships with more and more buyers.

Many firms do not invest in effective account planning and management to help drive account penetration. Anyone who has sold in this industry knows that the hardest part of the sales process is to break the ice with buyers and companies that are not familiar with you or the company.

Selling into existing accounts has the significant advantage of proven past performance that your sales people can leverage when reaching out to new buyers.

The ability to maintain and grow existing accounts requires different types of sales activities. Many people argue that it even requires a different type of sales person to do it effectively. There is truth on both accounts. The staffing manager has responsibility to ensure that the sales person is focused not only on making a placement today, but also in gaining a more in-depth understanding of their accounts. Some of the areas sales people may focus on include:

Understanding the company growth strategy: If a sales person knows how their clients make money today and how clients plan on making money in the future, he is better positioned to build strong new relationships. Being able to speak at some level of detail about the strategic direction of the company increases credibility and helps establish ongoing relationships.

Knowing the client's major projects: Companies invest in major initiatives for one or both of these reasons: 1) to drive revenue; 2) to increase profitability; Government regulation such as Sarbanes-Oxley adds a third and a fourth reason: 3) to stay out of jail; 4) to avoid fines. Regardless, projects drive spending, and knowing where the staffing needs are should determine where the sales person focuses their time and energy.

Awareness of compelling events: Mergers, bankruptcies, legislation, or any other event that may drive significant change within an organization may also drive hiring for contingent labor. Regardless of the tools, the more the sales people are aware of these types of events, the better they are prepared to adjust their sales activities to identify spend.

Understanding the organizational structure: Organizational charts are constantly in flux and can be difficult to assemble. Still, capturing where the buyers fit within an organization is critical in developing creative approaches to penetrate an account. Being able to recreate an organization chart is not enough. A sales person must strive to understand the dynamics of the relationships and how those relationships impact decision making within the organization.

Executing action items: Gathering this knowledge is useless unless the knowledge is supplemented by meaningful action items. The exercise of account planning encourages the staffing manager to manage their sales force differently. Instead of just measuring their sales people on metrics, managers need to incorporate specific objectives and coach their team on how to achieve those objectives. This is where account planning drives more productive behavior, while at the same time enhancing the skills of the sales team.

Part 2: Operational Alignment

As an operations manager, I was typically one of the first people in the office. This was my quiet time. It allowed me to prepare for the upcoming coverage meeting to evaluate the open job orders, coverage, pending interviews, and offers. Armed with this information I could objectively assign recruiters to work the positions that were most likely to close and bring in the most new gross profit dollars.

One day as I pulled into the parking lot, I noticed the cars of two sales people. I knew I was in for a confrontation. These sales people had low-priority positions and they were there to lobby their case. Once I got to my office, they explained to me how the recruiters were incompetent and not working hard enough to cover their job orders.

Calmly, I explained to them that job order volume was unusually high, and the problem with their job orders is that they were not as qualified as others that needed coverage. I then explained that my job was to maximize the new gross profit we were bringing in by focusing the team on the best job orders. My explanation went nowhere.

When they continued to demand that their job orders be made critical, my explanation was simple:

"Critical is not a feeling, it is an objective assessment of which clients have the best job orders for our company."

For all staffing managers out there, do not prioritize base on internal pressure. You need to know how and why your buyers hire, then prioritize your operations accordingly.

Making a company operationally competitive requires the constant attention of staffing managers. Operations are often overlooked because of the sales driven nature of the business. Companies ignore this issue to their own detriment. As the industry continues to become more competitive, effective operations is an absolute requirement for a staffing company's long-term survival. How effective are your operations? How do you measure that effectiveness? How do you determine what improvements need to be made to ensure your company remains competitive?

To answer those questions, one must define what is meant by operational alignment. At its basics, operational alignment is ensuring all the critical delivery processes are properly managed and supported to meet the client's buying criteria. These processes include:

- Job order management
- Sourcing
- Submittal management
- Assignment management.

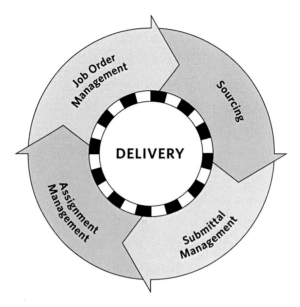

Like the sales strategy, operational alignment is ongoing. The process begins with job order management and then moves to sourcing and submittal management. Assignment management is also important to maintain contact with your candidates and can lead to future job orders and placements.

JOB ORDER MANAGEMENT

When I prepare for a meeting with a prospective staffing client, I look at their job order postings on their website. If the company diligently posts their jobs, the insight is invaluable. The number of jobs that are posted can be an indicator of company size. The geographical scope of the jobs can suggest the volume of jobs coming from VMS staffing programs. The variety of skill sets gives insight into the client's sales strategy. How long the postings have been open suggests how actively the company manages its job order queue.

Small staffing firms (<$10 million) with over 50 jobs (including administrative, legal, and IT) in various cities across the country immediately bring some concerns to mind:

- How does this firm compete with more focused firms?
- How can a small recruiting organization work such a variety of skill sets and locations?
- How will this firm scale?
- How is this firm building long-term value?

Poor job order management creates waste and inefficiencies. The nature of the job order queue determines how both recruiting and sales spend much of their time. If a firm is ineffective at job order management, the firm leaves the productivity of the team to chance.

Imagine the recruiting organization as a factory and the job order as a request from a client to build a product. Factories are most efficient when they can work on the same or closely related products over and over. Now, imagine a factory that is asked to build tractors one day and cars the next. Such production is impractical for many reasons, but for the purpose of this analogy, we will focus on three:

- Lack of inventory
- Lack of process
- Lack of expertise.

Lack of Inventory: To remain efficient, manufacturing companies must manage their demand. They understand that the more unpredictable demand is, the less productive their factories can be at making the product.

Now take the staffing organization that reacts to any demand and look at the potential impact that it has on operations. Recruiters can only maintain a finite amount of candidate inventory. The more repeatable the demand is, the easier it is for the recruiter to predict the needs of the client base. When recruiters are asked to work on a wide variety of skill sets and/ or locations, they cannot maintain an inventory. These recruiters then must rely on recruiting readily available talent that is often on the job boards. This dependency on public boards ultimately undermines the quality of available candidates and degrades the value a staffing company brings to the client.

Lack of Process: From a process perspective, recruiters must contend with different factors in sourcing, qualifying, and placing candidates for these positions. Some questions concerning process include:

Are the same job boards effective for all locations and skill sets?

Are there certifications or other requirements that must be verified?

Are some jobs higher risks than others from a worker's compensation perspective?

The lack of repeatable processes also complicates how recruiting management can hire and train new employees. Organizations with well-defined and focused processes have the flexibility to hire junior-level recruiters who can be plugged into a streamlined production desk.

Lack of Expertise: The lack of a focused, job order management process stretches the expertise of the team, forcing the team to work on positions they do not completely understand. This impacts the ability to qualify the job, to effectively source resumes, and to qualify the skills of the candidates. It also undermines the recruiter's ability to understand the motivations of the candidate and build the trust that encourages the candidate to take an offer if presented.

Never underestimate how job orders drive operations. Regardless of your stated strategy, a staffing company is defined by the clients it chooses to serve. Therefore, effective job order management ensures operations are properly focused and running at peak capacity. Organizations who manage job orders effectively have lower submittal-to-hire ratios, better responsiveness, and more productive teams.

Job order management is comprised of three specific processes which include:

- Job order qualification
- Job order prioritization
- Job order assignment.

Job Order Qualification

Just as you have to qualify the overall project opportunities for a company, you also have to qualify each individual job order. The purposes of job order qualification are first to determine whether the job should be added to the recruiting queue and second to gather data that helps determine how the job should be prioritized. Job order qualification can be broken into three areas: the job description, the level of urgency, and the hiring process.

Job description: The job description captures all the criteria necessary to match candidates to the job. Common areas of the job description include required and desired skills, duration of project, project description, job responsibilities, team composition, success factors, and compensation.

Level of urgency: The level of urgency is comprised of two parts: the timeline the position needs to be filled and the impact if the job is not filled on schedule. Positions become available for a variety of reasons. Some positions may merely be placeholders in a budget while others have a direct impact on a project being completed on time. Following are sample questions that can help establish the client's level of urgency in filling a position.

- Why is the position open?
- Is the position budgeted and approved?
- Describe the impact of the position on the project?
- When do you need the person to start?

Hiring process: The last area of job order qualification is defining the hiring process. Some clients have a disciplined process they follow for their hires, while others lack a consistent structure. For the former, staffing companies need to understand the process to set candidate expectations as well as gain further perspective on the urgency of the position. For hiring managers who do not have a hiring process, establishing a process for them can give your team an opportunity to differentiate itself from other staffing companies. Some questions to ask to better understand the process include:

- Who will be involved in the initial screening of the resumes?
- What will be the interview process?
- Are there any tests that will be used to screen for specific skills?
- What background checks will be required?

The information on qualifying job orders is not to provide a comprehensive one-size-fits-all approach. Instead, it should act as a starting point for the staffing manager to develop their own approach that suits the needs of their sales strategy and operations.

Job Order Prioritization

The purpose of prioritizing jobs is to maximize the new gross profit that can be generated by the company in both the short and long-term. Other considerations are more specific such as improving client diversification and supporting a new service offering.

There are two philosophies around how job orders are prioritized: laissez-faire and active management. Both viewpoints have their advantages and disadvantages. The approach a company decides to take is influenced by multiple factors that are unique to their circumstances.

Laissez-faire approach: The laissez-faire approach assumes that the production team is the best judge on what jobs need their focus. This approach can be effective if the team is structured in a way that drives clear accountability with consistent and productive collaboration. The best example of this is the "pod" structure. The pod structure assigns recruiters to a specific account manager. Typically, the account manager leads the group, but mutual accountability ensures job orders are qualified and prioritized effectively. This model can be very powerful, but its weakness lies in the effectiveness of the account manager to play a consistent leadership role in the group and/or whether the team has the business maturity to collaborate effectively. If either one of these two factors is broken, dysfunction is not too far behind.

Other laissez-faire approaches keep a recruiter in a neutral pool with little, if any, restrictions on what job orders they can work. This lack of structure, while easier to manage, has a host of problems that undermine efficiency including:

- Job orders being overworked by multiple recruiters
- New prospects being ignored by the recruiting team and undermining client diversification
- Account managers with strong personalities getting unbalanced attention
- Higher-margin business being ignored due to difficulty
- Creation of unhealthy account manager and recruiting cliques
- Unbalanced coverage.

Active management approach: Prioritization through active management relies on well-defined processes and the judgment of the recruiting manager to ensure the right jobs are being worked. The basic process steps encompass ranking the job order based on objective criteria, comparing the position to other open jobs, assigning the job order to a specific recruiter, following up on the progress against the job, and finally removing the job from the queue.

How a position moves through the queue depends on the client's buying patterns. An issue that is often overlooked by staffing managers is that they assume all clients purchase the same way. This assumption is patently false.

For example, some clients will only look at resumes that are received within a short period of time. For those clients, it does not matter that you respond with the best candidate 48 hours later. That candidate will never be seen by the client and much effort has been wasted. In cases like this, those jobs should be removed from the queue not based on submittal coverage, but based on time to ensure the queue is not contaminated with positions that are likely to have a low close rate.

There are other clients, who will continue to evaluate submittals throughout the hiring process. In those cases, your candidate still has the potential to be hired even if the candidate's material is submitted a few days later. Submittal coverage can be used when those jobs are removed from the sourcing queue.

Stages of prioritization include top priority to drive active sourcing while lower prioritization relies on passive sourcing. The next step is the removal from job order queue until sales receives feedback for existing submittals. The last step is completely closing out the job order from the pipeline.

Actively managing prioritization addresses the weaknesses of the laissez-faire approach. However, it also has weaknesses that must be taken into consideration:

- Management bandwidth can act as a bottleneck, reducing response time.
- Management can undermine collaboration between sales and recruiting.
- Management becomes overly involved in conflict resolution.
- Management may not have the skills, temperament, and experience to manage such a fluid environment.

The decision on how to prioritize jobs is an important one that must consider the sales strategy, the client base, and the experience level of the team. For this reason, a staffing company must weigh carefully all approaches, understand the consequences of the approach they choose, and manage accordingly.

Job Order Assignment

A couple of years ago, I was engaged by a company to iden-tify why close rates for job orders were rapidly decreasing. Part of the assessment was analyzing how job orders were assigned to recruiters. In this particular case, recruiters were assigned based on multiple factors such as past success with the client and the skill set requirements of the job.

When we opened the assignment report, a problem became im-mediately clear: Each recruiter was assigned anywhere between 12-14 jobs. In this particular staffing vertical, the most positions that typically should be worked are four to five.

When I asked why so many jobs were assigned, the response was "because that is how many we have open."

Job order assignment should be based on available recruiting bandwidth. Over-assignment does not improve coverage. Instead it overwhelms the recruiting desk, impacting quality and reducing close rates.

Job order prioritization and job order assignment are closely related. Prioritization takes objective criteria and allows the team to focus on the best jobs. Assignment is the process that matches the job orders to specific recruiters.

Many managers struggle with job order assignment. Common mistakes made by managers are assigning too many jobs, assigning jobs whose skill sets are too varied, and switching assignments too often. To become more effective at assigning positions, it is helpful to take an honest look at what activity you expect after a job order is assigned.

Recruiters who are assigned an order should actively work it. But what does that mean? For some recruiters, it may mean they post the job and then wait for responses, while others may shoot an email blast from the database or search LinkedIn.

The first approach exemplifies passive sourcing, which basically relies on candidates coming to the recruiter versus active sourcing where the recruiter is actively networking. Good recruiters use both techniques.

Remember that a recruiter can passively source for multiple positions, while at any time they can only actively source for one skill set, or possibly two or three, if they are closely related.

Many recruiting managers think that the number of job orders that a recruiter is assigned is based solely on how many jobs are currently available, which often is driven by the desire by sales to make sure every job gets a fair shake. This approach is both inefficient and counterproductive.

Instead, managers must take into consideration the following variables that impact the bandwidth of the recruiting desk:

- Type of sourcing required for each job
- Consistency of the skill sets
- Ability of the recruiter to multitask
- Capabilities of the Applicant Tracking System (ATS).

Much like prioritization, job order assignment can approached in many different ways. As a general rule, the more senior a recruiting team then the less structure needed in job order assignment. For more senior recruiters, it may be more effective to just assign them by client or skill sets or leave it entirely to their discretion. For junior recruiters, management may actively assign every job they work. The advantage of this approach is that you help the inexperienced recruiter focus on the right jobs, a skill that can take years to develop. A looser approach to job order assignment takes advantage of recruiter's experience to further qualify the job order. This eliminates the manager as a bottleneck and can make for a more streamlined process.

SOURCING

Sourcing includes the processes that provide accessible candidates' pools along with the available approaches to reach out and contact those candidates.

While many of the best practices in recruiting have remained stable over the last 20 years, sourcing has experienced revolutionary changes. These changes have not only altered how the recruiter runs his desk, but they also have enabled clients to move to a more transactional model with their staffing vendors increasing the pressure of commoditization.

For those new to the industry and/or who lack perspective of the scope of change that has occurred, imagine recruiting back in 1994. After you call your initial internal list and conducted networking calls, the next steps were very different. Email and online job boards did not exist in those days. Instead you would advertise the positions in the newspaper and wait until the next day. The most ambitious recruiters would show up early to see what gifts the thermal fax may have waiting for them.

Of course, sourcing is much different in today's world. Job boards, social networking sites, and email have changed both how we identify and contact prospective candidates. These tools have been so effective at broadening the visible pool of candidates that it has led many old-school staffing professionals to lament the death of the old-fashioned recruiting style built on networking and cold calling talent out of companies. That lament is misplaced because there are several niche staffing firms today who make traditional recruiting for high-value talent their primary differentiator, using today's technology to make them even more effective.

Is one recruiting style necessarily more effective than the other? That depends on the needs of the clients and how they want to be served. Any manager who believes he can rely on traditional sourcing methods to respond to the average VMS account is probably barking up the wrong tree for several reasons. First, VMS requirements can be too unpredictable to build a consistent network. Second, most VMS accounts require a response rate that precludes the ability to cold call talent out of companies. Third, the cost of traditional recruiting is expensive, and neither the margins nor productivity of the VMS business justify the cost.

As noted above, recruiting tactics must vary between each staffing firm based primarily on the needs of their clients. Staffing firms must take a more strategic view of how they organize their recruiting activities. While most firms focus on improving how they respond to active job orders, there can be significant returns in proactive sourcing if a staffing manager can identify predictability in skill sets, locations, compensation and seasonality. It is common for people to look at that list and contend such type of predictability does not exist in their business. Even though that might be correct, you should verify your assumptions by analyzing your past job orders.

If adding a proactive approach to your operations would be helpful, then the following steps can help you start a proactive recruiting approach.

Pipelining Repeatable Skills

Building discipline around repeatable skill sets can be an effective way to increase productivity, especially when dealing with large job order volume. For example, during the initial phases of supporting a VMS account, it is ideal to focus on the most repeatable and productive job orders instead of trying to cover all the jobs that are released. This enables proactive sourcing through leveraging job boards by constantly posting and searching for those repeatable skill sets helps to keep a fresh pipeline of readily available candidates. This process may require more investment in job boards, but if properly managed, that investment will pay for itself. Remember, staffing companies rely on talent; therefore, job boards are an investment in strengthening core capabilities.

Keeping the Database Updated

Effectively managing your candidate database allows you to segment out candidates who are actively looking versus the more passive population. Keeping your information current can be accomplished through marketing campaigns to incentivize candidates to update their profiles. Another option is to have dedicated sourcing headcount whose sole purpose is to keep the database fresh and relevant for the most marketable skill set.

Effectively Managing Offs

From my experience, most companies are ineffective at replacing contractors who are coming off assignment. Tracking and replacing contractors who are ending a project is low-hanging fruit for readily available talent. Firms that are good at replacing their candidates either have a strong employee relations department or work closely with the sales team to get up-to-date information on candidate status. These firms continually update their list of available candidates and make that list available to all recruiters and account managers for effective marketing.

Improve Lines of Communication

Improving how candidates are contacted for both passive and active sourcing can substantially increase recruiting productivity.

While the effectiveness of social media to drive candidate traffic has still yet to be proven, other avenues have been proven successful for generating different candidate pools.

Some examples of different communication techniques and where they can be effective are listed in the following table.

TECHNIQUE	AUDIENCE
Direct Phone Call	All candidates
Calling Software	Effective for most non-professional temporary labor
Mass Texting	Effective for professional and temporary, but must gain permission before using
Mass Emailing	Somewhat effective for professional, but effectiveness is diluted by spam filters
Newsletters	Can be an effective long-term sourcing strategy for niche professionals, not effective for immediate sourcing needs
LinkedIn Inmail	Effective for professional staffing when responsiveness is secondary
Other Social Media	TBD

It is also important to assess the sourcing activities in relation to different types of job orders. While the sourcing requirement for every company varies, answering the following questions can help identify improvements in your reactive sourcing approach:

- What tools do my recruiters have to identify and communicate with readily available talent?
- Are there repeatable skill sets or locations that we cannot respond to effectively?
- How long does it take recruiting to begin sourcing for a job order after it is received from the client?
- How long does it take before the position is posted?
- How are web applicants managed and how quickly are they vetted?

Improving sourcing processes requires understanding client buyer patterns and adjusting your approach accordingly. It is the staffing manager's role to guarantee the right investments and changes are made to both proactive and reactive sourcing to ensure the candidate pipeline remains competitive.

SUBMITTAL MANAGEMENT

It was only the first week of the month, and I was busy hanging another interview whiteboard. The number of client interviews was close to double our average amount. There was no question in my mind that we would have one of the strongest months the branch ever had. I showed that confidence to both my boss and the other branch directors at every opportunity so much that I am sure they were sick of hearing about it. I guess what happened next could be considered karma.

The interviews started dropping like flies. My interview-to-hire ratio tripled, and what could have been a historic month turned out to be well below average. I was eating crow with my team, my peers, and worst of all, my boss.

When I examined what happened, I realized that most of our candidates simply were not getting offers, and this was happening across all recruiters and all clients. What led to our increased ratio was a collective decision to take our eyes off the details. We all had so much activity <u>we cut corners on interview preparation</u> <u>and feedback.</u> From that day forward, I always kept my eye on the following items:

1. *High levels of activity can erode quality of critical processes.*
2. *Respect the amount of work required to get an interview and treat each appointment accordingly.*

The submittal process varies greatly from company to company for a variety of reasons. This section will discuss the variances from the qualification of the candidate to the point where the candidate is rejected or accepted by the client.

Years ago, when I decided to streamline recruiting processes, I knew I had to prioritize day-to-day recruiting activities first. I based the prioritization on two criteria: what value does the activity bring to the client, and what level of recruiting expertise was necessary to properly complete the activity. These criteria clarified that recruiting responsibilities can be segmented into three separate activities: sourcing, submittal management, and administrative.

The following table breaks down each of three activities that are typical for a recruiting desk. The bold items are activities that are both high value and require a significant level of expertise. As the chart shows, the submittal management is the one area that can provide the most value to the organization.

ACTION	ACTIVITIES OF RECRUITERS
Sourcing	• Job Posting • Job Board Searching • Database Maintenance • Mass Communication • **Networking** • **Cold Call Recruiting**
Administrative	• Resume Formatting • Job Posting • Benefits • Background Checks • Consultant Maintenance
Submittal Management	• **Candidate Qualification** • **Submittal Preparation** • **Interview Preparation** • **Presentation and Close**

To maximize the productivity of experienced recruiters, staffing managers need to find a way to maximize the time spent on high-value activities (bold) and minimize time on low-value activities (not bold). There are many ways staffing managers can reduce the time spent on low-value activities by using administrative support and automation. However, it also highlights the importance of effective submittal management in providing quality service to the client regardless if they have a VMS staffing program or working directly with the buyer.

By looking at the specific activities of submittal management, we recognize that it requires two high level skills: discernment and collaboration. Discernment is needed throughout the process from the initial qualification to knowing whether the candidate will take the job if offered. Collaboration is required to educate the account manager and the client on the merits of the candidate, especially if the candidate is not a perfect fit and then nego-tiating an offer that both sides can agree.

The importance of discernment and collaboration depends on how their clients buy. For low-access VMS accounts where candidates must get to the clients quickly, there is very little time for both steps. Staffing companies struggle with this fact, especially in a branch model where they are built to support both high-access local accounts and low-access VMS accounts.

As mentioned earlier, maintaining effective branch operations relies on consistency. Typically branches are built to support clients that value relationships with their vendors and expect a higher level of service. This value-added service is driven by the highly collaborative and client-focused approach a branch can provide.

When transactional VMS business is introduced into the branch, the collaboration that was a differentiator is now a competitive disadvantage. Recruiters try to adjust, but they find themselves having difficulty balancing the responsiveness requirements of the VMS with the expectation of quali-ty from the traditional clients. This leaves the branch operation stuck in the middle of the road begging to get run over by the competition.

Following are two sample interactions in which a recruiter presents a candidate to the account manager.

Scenario 1

Account Manager: *"What's up?"*

Recruiter: *"I just found a great candidate for your PM position."*

Account Manager: *"Great! Tell me about him. "*

Recruiter: *"He is a really good guy, I like him a lot. He has 15 years' experience in project management, 10 of which were in a manufacturing environment. "*

Account Manager: *"Sounds promising. Is he qualified and ready to go?"*

Recruiter: *"Yes, I just need to format the resume and I'll shoot it right over."*

Scenario 2

Account Manager: *"What's up?"*

Recruiter: *"I just found a great candidate for your PM position."*

Account Manager: *"Great! Has he been through the in-depth interview?"*

Recruiter: *"Yes, I just wrapped it up with him a few minutes ago."*

Account Manager: *"Was it face to face?"*

Recruiter: *"No, he is currently working and couldn't get away. I didn't want to slow down the process."*

Account Manager: *"Fair enough, talk me through the interview."*

Recruiter: *"He makes the same amount of money at the current project, but the situation is unstable and he is afraid the project may be pulled. He is open to about 25% travel."*

Account Manager: *"Okay, does he know that the travel occurs* in spurts?"

Recruiter: "I told him that some months there will be more travel than others, you know, especially at the beginning."

Account Manager: "What did he say?"

Recruiter: "He was okay with it."

Account Manager: "What are his primary motivators?"

Recruiter: "Well, obviously job security is a big factor, but he was also very excited with the fact that our client is growing so fast and investing in technology. He has been at the same place so long that he is a bit bored with it, and is concerned his skills are beginning to fall behind."

Account Manager: "Do you think there is flexibility in his rate? He may have a difficult time competing with other candidates because his technology is a bit dated."

Recruiter: "He seemed pretty adamant about the rate, but you never know. After he interviews there, he may become more flexible."

Account Manager: "How long has he been looking?"

Recruiter: "Six weeks. He had two interviews last week. He said they went well, but both clients have a fairly long list of candidates they are working through."

Account Manager: "Where does our opportunity rank?"

Recruiter: "Our job is a much better fit for him, and he seems to know it."

Account Manager: "When can he start?"

Recruiter: "He will give a standard two weeks, but would like to give three if possible."

Account Manager: "Why don't we get on the phone with him

> *together? I have some concerns about the travel, and he needs to know that his rate will be quoted up front – which may prevent him from getting an interview."*

While the second scenario seems more effective than the first, it really depends on the client. The first scenario is perfectly fine for a VMS client that has very little expectation for service. In contrast, the second scenario is far too slow for VMS, but is completely appropriate for direct access managers. It is the staffing manager's responsibility to define the process to meet the needs of their client's needs while being consistent with the company's value proposition.

> *As a rule of thumb, the higher the service level, the more structure is needed within the submittal management process to ensure quality levels are met.*

For staffing companies who sell quality directly to hiring managers, discernment and collaboration during the submittal management process must be at a high level.

Informed intuition or the ability to make the right decision with limited information relies heavily on repeated experiences that provide points of reference. This point of reference allows the recruiter to identify red flags and to understand the motivations of a specific candidate better. Applying that experience separates the experienced recruiter from the rookie. Processes and common language can reduce that gap, but nothing can fully replace it.

Collaboration between sales and recruiting brings the needs of the client and the realities of the candidate marketplace together allowing the team to produce a quality-driven solution. Well-defined processes and common language drive effective collaboration by clarifying expectations and strengthening communication between every member of the team.

However, where there is collaboration, conflict inevitably appears. Any staffing manager can attest to the underlying tensions between sales and recruiting. Conflicts are a natural part of collaboration and should not be completely avoided. After all, it is often through conflicts that the best solutions are created. If expectations are not defined and there is poor communication within the team, conflict can quickly become destructive. For this reason, the staffing manager must provide the processes and language for the teams to work effectively together.

There are two areas where consistent process and language can make an impact on submittal management: status updates and motivators.

Status updates: These updates capture the candidate status of their job search at any point in time. Status updates are fluid and must be reviewed frequently with the candidate. These reviews should focus on desired rate, availability to interview, availability to start, job submittals, and other interviews pending.

Recruiters and account managers need to discuss these items throughout the submittal management process. These matters become especially important after the client has committed to interviewing the candidate. At that point, the client needs to know the competitive landscape for the candidate. When armed with an accurate status update, the account manager can communicate to the client what is happening with the candidate's job search up front. This allows the account manager to better prepare the client for the interview as well as to avoid any embarrassing surprises.

Motivators: These simply capture what the candidate looks for in a job. This second area of candidate motivation tends to stay static unless a significant life event occurs.

It is important not to confuse motivators with the reason why a candidate is looking. As in the example above, the candidate is engaged in the job search because he is afraid his job will be eliminated. What the candidate actually seeks is a setting with better technology and also provides an opportunity to grow. Motivators can only be meaningful if they are compared to one another. For example, everyone wants more money, but are they willing to sacrifice money for better work hours and a shorter commute?

Some of the common motivators that the staffing manager can add to the qualification process are:

- Money
- Company culture
- Opportunity for advancement
- Commute
- Amount of travel.

After motivators are qualified, they should be referred to throughout the submittal management process. The motivators provide a negotiating tool for the recruiter when selling positions to the candidate, preparing the client for the interview, and eventually presenting the offer. Without defined motivators, recruiters tend to focus on compensation because money is always part of the negotiation. Negotiations become much more substantive when recruiters can focus on what the candidates really want, particularly when discussing an offer. If the candidate is looking for better technology, it is ineffective to close them on quality of the company café.

Effective negotiations begin and end with a clear understanding of what the candidate wants.

ASSIGNMENT MANAGEMENT

Assignment management covers the processes after a candidate is placed through the end of the assignment. Staffing firms vary widely on how they on-board and manage contractors. Regardless of variations, the process can be broken into four activities.

Documentation: The first activity centers on ensuring the candidate's paperwork is in order. This includes criminal checks, drug screenings, certification paperwork, benefit and tax paperwork, documents to validate approval to work, and payroll information.

Billing: The second activity is to ensure all the company invoicing information is captured accurately. This activity generates most of the invoicing errors because the sales person tends to underestimate the importance of an accurate invoice as part of the client experience.

Orientation: The third activity centers on providing orientation to the candidate to prepare the candidate for the assignment. Some companies choose not to have any type of orientation, especially if they are supporting national VMS staffing programs. In those cases there is not necessarily a lot a staffing firm can offer, because the staffing firm typically does not have much insight into the department or the projects the candidate will be supporting.

On the other hand, when a staffing firm has intimate knowledge of the client, an in-depth orientation can be very valuable. Information covered in an orientation can include the nature of the project, tips on working with the hiring manager, names of other contractors on the assignment, and any other tips on the culture or the logistics of working on the client site.

Maintenance: After a candidate gets started, ongoing consultant maintenance becomes the primary concern. As with on-boarding, the amount a staffing company invests in consultant maintenance varies widely. Some companies only provide logistical support, helping consultants with travel, payroll abnormalities, and benefits. Others take a more hands-on approach: focusing on employee morale and keeping close tabs on the progress of the assignments.

Some staffing managers mistakenly assume a more engaged consultant maintenance program is only relevant for local non-VMS accounts. That is a bad assumption. Often, staying actively engaged with the consultants at a VMS account provides incredible value. By developing strong relationships with billing contractors, account managers gain insight on the state of the project, the culture of the department and what positions may become available. When you do not have access to the hiring managers, this information can lead to a significant competitive advantage.

Part 3: Performance-Driven Culture

> *There is a great line in the movie <u>Remember the Titans</u> when a player is challenged by the captain of the team. According to the captain, the player was a waste of God-given talent, and it was his selfish, negative attitude that held him back and hurt the team. The player did not deny his bad attitude; instead, he threw it back at the captain with three simple words:*
>
> *"Attitude reflects leadership."*

Like competitive sports, much of the success of a staffing company boils down to individual performance and a motivated team. Staffing managers must develop a Performance-Driven Culture that strives for excellence, and rewards hard work and individual accountability. A strong performance culture mitigates the negative forces that impact employee attitudes towards their jobs. The attitude of a team is a reflection of the company leadership especially in uncertain times. So how are business leaders doing?

The 2010 annual job satisfaction survey conducted by the national organization The Conference Board[2] recently released results on employee satisfaction and revealed that only 45% of employees are satisfied with their jobs. That is the lowest level in the 23 years the poll has been conducted. Certainly market conditions bear much of the responsibility. Leaders have been forced to make very difficult decisions including layoffs, salary,

---

[2] Ray, Rebecca and Rizzacasa, Tom. "Job Satisfaction Survey," The Conference Board, 2011

and benefit cuts while at the same time asking their employees to do more with less to maneuver successfully through the latest recession. These changes, especially if poorly managed, can cause substantial damage to the company culture and the relationship between employees and management. While the 2012 survey indicates slight improvement, the levels of satisfaction are still alarmingly low.

Many leaders may look at their high employee retention rate and assume they do not have a problem. However, even with a 55% dissatisfaction rate, The Conference Board results show only 19% of employees are looking for other jobs. This suggests that retention is not reliable barometer of employee attitudes. Why the disconnection? Why are unhappy employees staying? The biennial Global Workforce Study[3] of employee attitudes and workplace trends by Towers Watson suggests that employees are choosing security over career satisfaction. In the end, many employees are staying, not because they believe in their company, but because they are too afraid to leave. While this helps with retention, this attitude does not drive performance. It only suggests employees will work hard enough not to get fired.

To foster a positive team attitude, a leader needs to reduce the influence generated by fear and uncertainty and replace that with a laser focus on performance and future growth. The first step in accomplishing this is for leaders to understand what their team needs in terms of leadership. The Global Workforce Study provides insight into this concern:

"Given the state of affairs in many businesses over the last year, per-

---

[3] Towers Watson, <u>2010 Global Workforce Study</u>, 2010

haps it shouldn't come as a surprise that trustworthiness tops the list of desired senior leadership qualities," said Caldwell. "This craving for the more 'emotionally intelligent' aspects of leadership indicates that many employees feel disconnected from their organization and are looking for their leaders to project integrity and empathy, and continue to focus on the development of employees. " His research has found that employees look for these characteristics in their managers:

- Is trustworthy: 79%
- Cares about the well-being of others: 67%
- Encourages the development of talent in the organization: 56%
- Is highly visible to employees: 42%
- Manages financial performance successfully: 42%.

Keep in mind that this is not a call to coddle underperforming employees. Rather, it provides context on how leaders can communicate their vision, as well as support and motivate their team. People want to be led, but they expect active engagement, effective communication, and leaders that are willing to invest in their development.

For staffing managers, the impact of employee dissatisfaction on company culture cannot be overstated. There are many companies that have compelling services as well as a strong client base and good people, but have a weak culture that undermines performance. Understanding your performance culture is required to determine what changes are needed to make a team more effective. The first step is to determine the drivers of a company sales culture and to identify the threats to its effectiveness.

WHAT IS CULTURE?

Before we dive too far into the drivers of a culture, we must understand what culture is and how it impacts team productivity. Company culture can be described as a set of unwritten rules that determine employee behavior and decision making. Culture determines what is appropriate and inappropriate for interactions between employees, their managers, and clients. Measuring the impact of an effective culture is very difficult, but anyone who has witnessed both high-performance and low-performance organizations understands its impact on company effectiveness.

A variety of internal and external drivers influence company culture. As these drivers go through change, so does the company's culture. As a staffing manager, understanding the cultural impact of these drivers can prove elusive. Additionally, understanding the impact allows you to make adjustments to how you manage to make certain the Performance-Driven Culture is not eroded slowly by internal and external factors.

Team composition: The seniority of a team can have a significant impact on the type of culture leadership that may develop. If an organization chooses to change its hiring profile, then it should look at the current company culture and determine what changes need to occur in order for that profile to be successful. Hiring people to change the company culture without proper preparation is a common mistake that leaders make which can lead to higher employee turnover and decreased performance.

Strategic drivers: How the sales strategy and operational alignment are defined have a significant impact on the culture. In general, organizations which have highly structured processes that are heavily managed tend to be more transactional in nature. This drives a very high-paced culture that focuses primarily on high activity levels. Organizations with looser processes tend to desire greater collaboration and problems solving between team members. In these organizations, activity is often secondary to quality which leads to a more intentional quality focused culture.

Management style: The management styles which leadership employs impact the company culture both through their personalities as well as the management tactics they decide to use. For example, management styles that are very forceful and intrusive may not be consistent with a company that needs the sales team to take risks and drive innovative approaches to the market. This inconsistency between management style and success factors can confuse the team and lead to low employee morale.

In addition to the internal drivers above, there are specific policies and processes that are linked to the culture such as the hiring strategy, performance management, and compensation. The rest of the chapter will focus on the cultural impact of each of these.

HIRING STRATEGY

One of the most common questions from staffing managers is whether it is better to hire experienced or green sales people. Leveraging my years of experience, I can confidently answer that I really do not know. I have come to this conclusion because I have seen both profiles succeed and fail. In the end, I believe experience level is a poor predictor of performance. This assertion is supported by a study conducted by American psychologists Frank Schmidt and John Hunter[4], who discovered that basing hiring

---

[4] Schmidt, Frank L. and Hunter, John E., "The Validity and Utility of Selection Methods in Personnel Psychology: Practical and theoretical implications after 85 years of research findings," American

decision on experience level had only slightly better results than a coin flip or handwriting analysis. Neither of these tactics is terribly effective.

I am not suggesting that experience should be completely discounted because the level of experience should play an important role. However, in screening candidates, experience should be balanced by those difficult to define qualities that drive the focus and perseverance of most successful sales people.

In their book *Never Hire a Bad Sales Person*, Dr. Christopher Croner and Richard Abraham[5] leverage years of data to capture personality characteristics that are consistent with top producers. The compilation of these characteristics is what they refer to as Drive. Drive is that persistent motivation focused on winning and, according to the authors, is the most critical criterion for hiring performers. The authors suggest three components of Drive: the need for achievement, the desire to compete, and eternal optimism about success.

The need for achievement: Great sales people measure themselves on their achievements and have natural discipline and focus to reach their goals. Discipline and focus are not always easy to recognize. Often sales people seem anything but disciplined. After all, how many sales people really know how to use a CRM and are effective at ensuring the information is complete? Keep in mind, the sales person's discipline is focused on achievement and sees data entry as a formality taking away time needed for success.

Psychological Association, 1998

[5] Croner, Christopher and Abraham, Richard. *Never Hire a Bad Salesperson Again: Selecting Candidates Who Are Absolutely Driven to Succeed*, The Richard Abraham Company, LLC; 2006

The desire to compete: Good sales people believe in winning and constantly compare themselves to their competition. This competitiveness can manifest itself as a bull in a china shop, bringing with it unique management challenges. A good sales manager can help focus that energy in a positive way while at the same time understanding that destructive behavior needs to be addressed aggressively to keep the culture from becoming dysfunctional.

Eternal optimism: They believe they will win regardless of the rejections and failures they experience – success is just around the corner. This type of optimism is a rare gift and, when combined with the previous characteristics, gives the sales person the emotional runway to overcome failure. This optimism is also strengthened by the fact that they do not take defeat personally. They do not beat themselves up when they fail. Instead, they move onto the next opportunity with the same optimism that they had pursuing the previous one.

While drive is an important component of hiring good producers, drive will not make up for a hire that is a bad cultural fit. There are plenty of producers who have terrific drive, but whose values and temperament are poisonous to a productive culture. While this type of producer is very capable of running their own desk, they will negatively influence the culture and thus undermine management's credibility and authority.

Another approach to hiring people who are consistent with your culture is to use tests such as Myers-Briggs Type Indicator, DISC Assessment, or Birkman Method. Each of these takes different approaches to identify strengths and predict behavior. Using these tools effectively requires a level of expertise, so a certified consultant is strongly recommended.

While a manager can use formal methodologies to hire talent, there really is no guarantee that the person you hire will be the same person who shows up to work. When a company hires experienced sales people, risk increases because they are not only the face of the company to the market, but they are more difficult to evaluate because they are expected to be out of the office. I have worked with companies that have held onto supposed rainmakers for over a year, waiting to be flooded with money, but to eventually find out that that sales person was not a rainmaker at all.

Ineffective hiring is a very expensive lesson for the staffing manager to learn and provides much of the explanation as to why more and more firms are hiring junior recruiters and promoting them into sales. Hiring junior employees (0-2 years out of school) requires that managers pay especially close attention to the first 60 to 90 days of employment. During this time, they need to establish metrics and provide a consistent review process to confirm the new hire is progressing as planned. After the first few months, they will be ready for the second process that influences the performance culture: performance management.

PERFORMANCE MANAGEMENT

Early in my career, our firm grew out of our executive office space and expanded into new quarters about three times the size. My new office was located in front, allowing me to see the comings and goings of all the employees.

I made a series of new hires, one of whom was a junior-level recruiter that was the daughter of an executive of one of our clients. I do not consider myself to be a micromanager, but the location of my office allowed me to see details about my employees that I may otherwise not have noticed.

One of the things that became clear was how many smoke breaks this new hire took in a given day. I would estimate she took a break two or three times an hour, with each break taking about five to ten minutes. As a manager, this drove me crazy, especially since her performance was well below minimum expectations.

Finally, when I was feeling especially impatient and she was heading for another smoke break, I immediately called her into my office. She came in wondering what was going on and I told her that she was taking too many smoke breaks and she needed to cut back. She proceeded to cry in my office telling me how it was not any of my business how much she smokes. I explained that my concern was the impact on her productivity, not on her health. Well, that did not go well.

She quit and we lost the client leaving me with two lessons:

- *Don't hire your client's kids.*
- *Don't try to ad lib performance management.*

One of the strengths of the industry is the focus on individual productivity. This focus has made one-on-one performance management a relative strength for many staffing companies and formal performance reviews a fairly common element of many existing management frameworks. While performance management is taking place, it often is ineffective since management is not sure what they are trying to accomplish during performance reviews. The purposes for performance management are these:

- To set performance and hold the producer accountable to specific performance expectations
- To coach the producer on how to improve their performance
- To assess the producer's development.

The formality of the review and how much it crosses over into other topics depends on the culture that management tries to encourage. Some companies view performance reviews as very one-sided and dominated by the manager, while others view performance reviews as more of a collaborative session where a variety of topics are covered.

The frequency of the review also varies from company to company. As a rule of thumb, if the staffing manager wants to achieve all three objectives, the reviews have to be done at least quarterly. If the staffing manager decides to only conduct reviews semi-annually or annually then the only value of the performance review is to make human resources feel better. In order to accomplish more from your reviews, then the following guidelines could be useful:

- Develop consistent metrics for each production group.
- Give each producer different targets reflecting their circumstance.
- Make sure the producer comes in prepared to give their perspective on their performance.
- Document specific objectives that focus on areas the producer needs to improve.
- Be direct and constructive with both criticism and praise.

While performance reviews take a significant amount of time, they are the most direct and effective way to establish and maintain a Performance-Driven Culture. Performance reviews assert this influence through effective communication, one-on-one coaching, and clear expectations. If staffing managers choose not to conduct those reviews, they will see their influence wane as the organization grows – and potentially lose control of the culture they tried so hard to establish.

Even if a staffing company has an excellent hiring process and is effective with performance management, none of it will matter if the company has poor incentive policies. Incentives include compensation plans and other monetary and non-monetary awards.

COMPENSATION PLANS

Of all the things that influence the Performance-Driven Culture, the compensation plan is the one area that gets the most attention. Staffing managers see compensation as the most powerful lever to influence the behavior of their producers. However, it is important for staffing managers to understand that compensation is just part of a wider effort to developing a Performance-Driven Culture and compensation cannot stand on its own.

The effectiveness of a compensation plan can be linked directly to how well that plan is aligned with the company sales strategy. The sales strategy influences compensation for both sales and recruiting by defining the following:

- The financial model of the business
- The different sales roles and how they are compensated
- How best to compensate recruiting roles
- How the payout is distributed between sales and recruiting.

Understanding the amount of gross profit available for compensation is an important starting point when staffing managers develop commission plans. Too often, staffing managers choose from other companies' plans without realizing their financial model may be significantly different from their competitors. One of the biggest variables is gross profit percentages where you can see significant variability between different firms within the same staffing vertical.

There can also be significant variability on the Selling, General and Administration (SG&A) costs depending on the structure of the organization (branch vs. centralized), services provided, and the overall productivity of the business. The only way to know the financial model is for the staffing manager to work with the CFO and forecast different scenarios based on projections from the current account list. For more detail on gross profit and SG&A see Chapter 4 as well as the glossary of terms at the end of the book.

After the staffing manager has a strong grasp on the gross profit available for compensation, they are ready to determine how that gross profit will be distributed between the sales and recruiting organizations.

A company with a well-defined sales strategy has a much easier time understanding the objectives of its compensation plans. Even with that clarity there can be a tendency to over engineer the compensation plan in an attempt to cover all the strategy's objectives. This tendency can be linked to management's desire to have the compensation plan play a larger role in driving and managing behavior than it can effectively influence. Instead management must focus on the one or two most important elements of the job description and build a plan according.

Staffing managers are notoriously sloppy at defining the job descriptions of their producers to match their strategic goals. The dominant thinking is staffing is a simple business; therefore, spending too much time on such things overcomplicates the obvious. Nothing could be further from the truth, especially when discussing the sales force. Even a basic difference such as the role of the farmer versus the hunter brings in a host of questions that need to be answered when developing a plan.

As an example, many organizations pay a percentage of the gross profit that the sales person "generates." Is it in the company's interest to pay the same override to an account manager who can rarely, if ever, influence the buying process than one who continually hunts and brings in new business? Do both sales people bring the same value, and are both as difficult to replace? The answer should be an emphatic "no", but far too often the staffing manager compensates the positions the same way even though it is obvious the positions differ radically.

I strongly recommend the book *Compensating the Sales Force* by David Cichelli[6] for any staffing manager looking to evaluate compensation plans. In his book, Cichelli does an excellent job of breaking down the different types of sales positions, many of which are very relevant to today's staffing company.

The following table shows each role and how that role manifests itself in a staffing company.

---

[6] Cichelli, David. *Compensating the Sales Force: A practical guide to designing winning sales reward programs*, McGraw-Hill, 2010

ROLE	RELEVANCE TO STAFFING
Demand Creation	Focuses on stimulating the marketplace to create interest in the company. This is traditionally the role of marketing, but often is a secondary role for both the account manager and hunter.
Buyer Identification	Buyer identification is the centerpiece for the hunter. Account managers with a license to hunt are also responsible for this role.
Purchase Commitment	As with buyer identification this is about access and influence. Can the sales person influence the buying process and, if so, how much more business can be generated by that influence?
Order Fulfillment	Job order and submittal management can come to dominate a sales person's time. Is that time a true differentiator that brings value to the client, and provides a competitive edge to the staffing firm?
Customer Service	Consultant and client maintenance, while potentially valuable, take time away from closing new sales. Is your sales team becoming expensive customer service reps? Does customer service allow them to close business?

Depending on the nature of the operations, there can be significant variance of responsibilities within the recruiting organization as well. Some of the variations are:

- Branch versus centralized
- Sourcing recruiters versus submittal management recruiters
- Onshore versus offshore full life cycle recruiting
- Offshore sourcing versus onshore submittal management
- Both onshore and offshore full life cycle
- VMS versus non-VMS.

Each one of these models represents different job descriptions and also different cost models which must be taken into consideration by the staffing manager. For example, if a staffing manager decides to pay for dedicated sourcing recruiters, what is the impact to the compensation for the recruiters that are responsible for submittal management? Does the increase in production call for the staffing manager to pay the traditional recruiter a lower percentage of the gross profit?

Defining how the total gross profit is distributed between sales and recruiting is an important consideration before you begin developing a compensation plan. The distribution between the two groups should be based on the following criteria:

- The difficulty of recruiting new talent into the role
- The importance of retention
- The need to recognize who holds subject matter expertise
- The operational demands of the clients.

Outside of motivating the right behaviors, recruiting and retention are the other two main objectives of a compensation plan. Most staffing managers are looking to recruit "top-notch" sales people and are willing to pay well for them. The business driver of this need typically is a mixture of top-line growth and diversification, very important and justifiable reasons to pay top dollar for the right sales person. However, the problem is in the assumptions. First, that a top performer at one company will be a top performer in another. Second, that there are enough top performers who are willing to leave their current company around whom to build a team.

Staffing managers who use those assumptions can build a compensation plan with large salaries and/or draws that attract marginal talent. Instead, most staffing managers will have to settle for junior to mid-level talent, which given the right opportunity and environment can develop into productive members of the team.

> *The staffing manager who masters the ability to hire and develop high-talent/low-experience employees will have a long and very prosperous career.*

Another consideration in determining how gross profit is distributed focuses on where the subject matter's expertise lies within the staffing company. Some firms have senior-level sales people working with junior recruiters, and others have it the other way around, while still others strive for a balance between the two.

In the branch model, the expertise typically lies within the sales organization or balances the expertise between the two teams. If the expertise is dominated by the sales organization, then the recruiting team can be composed of more junior-level producers. In some settings, this goes as far as having recruiters report to specific sales people which has proven to be very successful based on the size of some of the firms that use that model. In that case, it is perfectly justifiable to pay a larger percentage of the gross profit to the sales person because they are providing expertise and leading the critical processes.

On the other side of the spectrum, VMS accounts that prohibit access may best be served by a model where the expertise resides within the recruiting team. In this case, the recruiter probably has an executive sponsor to handle escalation, but the day-to-day sales role is more along the lines of customer service than driving the process. In that case, a senior recruiter that can source and manage submittals for multiple positions provides the expertise and the differentiation. In those cases, paying a recruiter a larger percentage of the gross profit is reasonable.

The last consideration in determining the distribution of the gross profit is the operational demands of your clients. Highly productive accounts with low submittal-to-hire ratios and strong job order close rates can support one recruiter per sales person. In those cases, the staffing manger typically pays the individual sales person a higher percentage of the gross profit per deal leading to more of the total gross profit to be paid out to the sales organizations.

Unfortunately, those types of ratios are rare in staffing today. It is not unusual for submittal-to-hire ratios to be 18:1 and for close rates to be in the low to mid-teens. These ratios demand a lower cost per submittal, and/ or greater operational throughput than one recruiter can provide per sales person. Staffing managers must understand what operational throughput is required and allocate gross profit to the sales and recruiting organizations accordingly.

For creative staffing companies, compensation is more than just salary and commissions. These companies also look towards other incentives both monetary and non-monetary to recognize performance. Sales trips, top performer clubs, and non-monetary awards are all effective ways to recognize performance outside of the core compensation package.

Some of the reasons a staffing firm may consider other incentives are:

- Change company strategy
- Reward critical activity (leads, new accounts)
- Build a strong team
- Fight complacency.

To fully comprehend the role of compensation within the Performance-Driven Culture, it is necessary for staffing managers to appreciate the role of recognition in a production environment.

> *Sales people and recruiters face rejection, complaints, and uncertainty on a daily basis. Recognition – whether it is financial or not – fuels motivation and gives them the incentive they need to reach their potential.*

Even if a company has the right hiring profiles, incentives, and performance management, the culture can still be undermined if management is ineffective at engaging employees. It is well documented that employee satisfaction is directly linked to their relationship with a manager.

From the employee perspective, the relationship with their manager can be a complex one. They often see themselves as dependent on the manager's judgment, and look to their managers for both respect and guidance. It is the manager's job to effectively assert authority, while at the same time keeping the team motivated. There are plenty of managers who can successfully motivate their employees through authority alone. The majority of managers feel more comfortable with a more collaborative management philosophy.

Culture defines the unwritten rules of behavior and it is those unwritten rules that truly define how well a team works together. While developing a Performance-Driven Culture often is seen as touchy feely leadership, the performance culture is the "x" factor in staffing company performance and is largely influenced by how you manage.

The impact of processes and policies on the culture should be a significant topic when any changes are considered. If changes are contrary to the current culture, then they will fail. If the changes are consistent with the culture, they will succeed. While all policies and processes impact the culture, hiring strategies, performance management, and compensation are built specifically for their cultural impact and should be viewed accordingly.

Wrapping Up

In order to drive the intended financial results the staffing manager must ensure that the strategic drivers are both individually strong and aligned with one another. The sales strategy focuses on all the necessary elements that bring job orders to the delivery organization. Effective operational alignment ensures the delivery capabilities meet the needs of the targeted buyers. The Performance-Driven Culture captures the elements that ensure the team is naturally motivated to the right behaviors.

Managing to improvements and alignment within each of these drivers requires experience, discipline, and a well-defined, knowledgeable approach. Without that experience, knowledge, and discipline, staffing managers either do nothing to improve their operations or cause more harm than good with poorly defined improvements. But even if improvements are not required, the staffing manager must stay actively engaged to ensure there is proper alignment between the three drivers.

Alignment is not a natural state for an organization and can be undermined even by a seemingly positive event. The most common example of this is when a staffing company lands a large account. This is typically seen as a positive event, but too often the staffing managers underestimate the impact a large and demanding client can have on both operational alignment and culture. The staffing manager assumes all new business is good business while processes break, confusion spreads, and morale atrophies.

Strong staffing managers understand the capabilities of their strategic drivers, and can appreciate how they must adapt to meet new challenges. The focus of this chapter was to define the drivers so you can begin asking the right questions on the state of your operations, but this is a small step. To gain a greater appreciation for the importance of the drivers, the staffing manger must also understand the relationship between financial performance and the strategic drivers.

Chapter 4:
Financial Impact

During the 1990s, our company was growing at an incredible pace. We had opened three successful offices, each of which had double-digit revenue growth. To fuel this growth, we continued to hire and reward our top revenue producers with awards and rich compensation plans. Why worry about our sales and recruiting costs when revenues kept climbing? Well, the new millennium was approaching and we were about to discover there was plenty to worry about.

Our focus on headcount and revenue growth blinded us to gross profit pressures that were coming from our largest accounts. These pressures became clear once the volume discounts started being deducted, and both our gross profit percentage and net income declined.

> *It seems that closing low-margin business and paying increasingly higher placement bonuses is a bad way to make money. In fact, we lost money on many placements we made at our largest client. The executive team quickly made adjustments to our burden and compensation plans. While this shook up the team, it provided an expensive, but important lesson.*
>
> *Revenue is just the window dressing. Gross profit is the true measure of growth.*

The financial model provides you important insight needed on the short and long-term health of your business. For some, the financial oversight of the business is the most painful part, requiring significant attention to detail and constant scrutiny. You will have greater success in this area if you have some basic information to help you to focus on the most important areas for staffing.

Fundamentals

There are three types of financial reports commonly used to measure a staffing operations performance: the balance sheet, the cash flow statement, and the income statement.

The income statement or Profit and Loss statement (P&L) is the most common financial report used by line-level staffing managers. On the other hand, ownership must focus on all three reports to determine the overall financial health of the organization. This chapter will give a brief summary of the balance sheet and the cash flow statement, but the focus will primarily be on the P&L and how it relates to staffing.

The **Balance Sheet** provides executives insight into the financial health of the company at a specific point in time. Balance sheets need to be compared over time to see if the financial position of the company is improving. The balance sheet takes into consideration assets, liabilities, and owner's equity. Assets consist of anything of value including cash, receivables, and fixed assets. Liabilities are financial obligations from past events, such as payroll, accounts payables, or loan payables. Owner's equity captures what is left over for the shareholders. Owner's equity includes the amount invested by the owners plus the profits or minus the losses. The formula that defines the balance sheet is:

Assets = Liabilities + Owner's Equity

The balance sheet derives its name from the fact that the assets must balance with the liabilities and owner's equity, even if it produces negative owner's equity which means that you owe more than the company's assets are worth. Over time, you want to see the owner's equity increase as the financial strength of the company improves.

The following graphs show the balance sheet over time in two different scenarios. In Company A the revenues are growing each year while the liabilities are increasing at a faster rate, thus the owner's equity decreases. In Company B the revenues remain relatively flat while liabilities decrease; therefore, the owner's equity improves. As these two scenarios show, it is important to analyze gains in revenue along with the impact on liabilities and owner's equity.

Balance Sheets of Two Firms

Company A

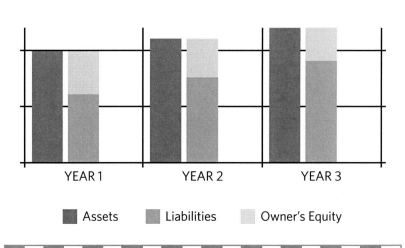

YEAR 1   YEAR 2   YEAR 3

■ Assets   ■ Liabilities   ■ Owner's Equity

Company B

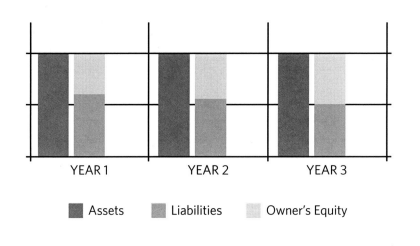

YEAR 1   YEAR 2   YEAR 3

■ Assets   ■ Liabilities   ■ Owner's Equity

The Cash Flow Statement is primarily a measure of a company's short-term viability. The cash flow statement is for a period of time such as a month, quarter, or year, and shows the inflow and outflows of cash and the net change in cash for the period. The tracking of cash flows provides insight into the company's ability to pay its obligations, including payroll. Companies that have low profitability and have trouble collecting their receivables tend to struggle with cash flow and have to rely on lines of credit to fund operations. On the flip side, highly profitable firms with low receivables can often fund their own payroll and save on interest payments.

The following graph shows the impact of a single placement on cash flow for a six-month period. If you assume a 60-day receivable agreement where the contractor works a total of four months, the staffing company must fund the payroll for the first two months before seeing any payment

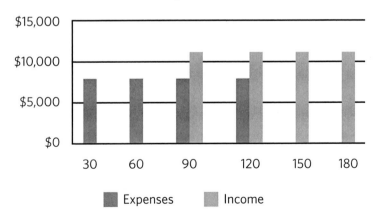

Cash Flow of 60-Day Receivable Placement

from the client. The staffing company continues to receive payments for two months after the contract has ended for the consultant. Because of the impact on cash flow, the gross profit for each placement is important to the financial stability of the company.

Another important factor in cash flow is how rapidly the staffing company is growing. Fast-growing staffing companies can run into cash problems while shrinking staffing companies can be flush with cash. A fast-growing staffing firm is adding new consultants, which will require payroll obligations before the client pays for the consultants. In these situations, a staffing company may have to access a line of credit, or if necessary, factor their receivables to fund payroll. In a shrinking company, there are not as many payroll obligations and they should have cash coming in from prior placements to help fund the declining payroll.

The **Income Statement** captures a line-by-line summary of financial

STAFFING COMPANY INCOME STATEMENT	
Revenue	$20,000
Direct Costs (Salary/Taxes/Benefits paid to consultants)	$14,940
Gross Profit Dollars	$5,060
Gross Profit Percentage ($5,060/$20,000)	25.3%
Total SG&A Costs (Staff Compensation/ Occupancy/Job Boards/etc.)	$4,260
Operating Profit or EBITDA (Revenue - Direct Costs - SG&A Costs)	$800
Operating Profit % ($800/$20,000)	4.0%

performance over a period of time. The income statement begins with top line performance and reveals how expense items lead to net income.

Years ago, most staffing companies would evaluate a P&L by measuring revenue for top-line growth and EBITDA (Earnings before Interest, Taxes, Depreciation, and Amortization) for profitability. Today's manager must focus on two things: gross profit growth and internal compensation expenses. While there are other things that impact the financial health of a staffing company, as a general rule, if gross profit consistently grows and the cost of their staff remains reasonable, healthy profits will follow.

In order to determine the P&L for a staffing firm, you need to know how to calculate revenue for contract placements. Revenue can be explained as the compilation of the bill rates multiplied by the number of total hours worked. In the following chart, in order to calculate monthly revenue for Company 1, you multiply 10 contractors x $70/hr x 160 hours worked = $112,000.

CALCULATION OF MONTHLY REVENUE				
	Number of Contractors	Bill Rate	Hours Worked in Month	Total Monthly Revenue
Company 1	10	$70/hr	160	$112,000
Company 2	8	$65/hr	160	$83,200

THE GROSS PROFIT CALCULATION

Another important term on the P&L for staffing firms is gross profit. The terms "gross profit" and "gross margin" are used interchangeably, but I will use the term gross profit for consistency. There are two ways to look at gross profit: one is actual gross profit dollars (GP$s) and the other is a percentage of revenue (GP%). Each is important in understanding the financial health of the business.

Gross Profit Dollars (GP$s) = Revenue - Direct Cost of Employing Contractors

For contract placements, Gross Profit Dollars simply subtracts the direct costs of employing the contractors from that number. The largest direct cost is the pay rate. However, there are employment taxes (Social Security, Medicare) and benefit costs (healthcare, 401K) that need to be added to the pay rate to get the burdened rate. Many times, the production team is given a percentage burden to estimate the gross profit of each deal. The percentage burden is provided so producers can quickly calculate their commissions on any given placement. This visibility into gross profit at the producer level is critical to motivate the team to negotiate profitable business.

Gross Profit Percentage (GP%) = Gross Profit/Revenue

Gross Profit Percentage (GP%) shows how much gross profit is generated relative to the revenue. This is especially useful as a macro measurement of a branch's financial health. The higher the GP%, the better the cash flow and the ability to of the staffing company to acquire the line of credit it may need.

Both the gross profit dollars and gross profit percentage are critical factors for a fast-growing staffing firm that must float money between the time it pays consultants and when the firm gets paid by the client. Staffing operations succeed or fail based on their ability to add healthy gross profit year over year. The importance of focusing on gross profit continues to increase as buyers squeeze margins and worker's compensation claims escalate.

The following chart provides a clear example of how important gross profit can be when analyzing different clients. If you measure the clients on only revenue, it gives the false impression that Client A outperforms Client B by 25%. When one considers gross profit, it is clear that Client B produces a higher gross profit percentage and over 8% more gross profit dollars.

ANALYZE REVENUE AND GROSS PROFIT BY CLIENT			
Company	Monthly Revenue	Gross Profit Percentage	Total Gross Profit/Mth
Client A	$8,000	18%	$1,440
Client B	$6,000	26%	$1,560

Assuming the SG&A to support each account is comparable, Client B will contribute significantly more to the bottom line. The advantages of Client B become clearer when cash flow is taken into consideration. Because most staffing companies must pay the consultant before they get paid by the client, the gap between revenue and gross profit reflects how much money a staffing company must pay upfront to receive the revenue. In essence, the lower the gross profit percentage, the lower the return on floating the consultant's pay. Companies with low gross profit percentages are more vulnerable to delays in receivables and are more reliant on lines of credit to finance their operations.

The gross profit is also important when analyzing each placement. The following chart shows the impact of lowering the burdened rate from $50 per hour to $45 per hour. With the $5 reduction in the burdened rate, the staffing company can reduce their cash flow by $800 each month. While this may not seem like a significant amount, if you expand this trend to over 100 consultants then the effect to cash flow is substantial. In addition, the $5 lower rate amounts to an increase in gross profit of 25% over the course of a four-month contract.

EFFECT ON GROSS PROFIT OF LOWERING BURDENED RATE BY $5/HR				
Placements	Burdened Rate	Bill Rate	Paid to Contractor Monthly	Due from Client Monthly
Placement 1	$50/hr	$70/hr	$8,000	$11,200
Placement 2	$45/hr	$70/hr	$7,200	$11,200
GROSS PROFIT FROM SAME TWO PLACEMENTS				
Placements	Burdened Rate	Bill Rate	Gross Profit Earned Monthly	Gross Profit Earned over 4-Month Contract
Placement 1	$50/hr	$70/hr	$3,200	$12,800
Placement 2	$45/hr	$70/hr	$4,000	$16,000

SG&A COSTS

While evaluating business based on gross profit can be informative, there are times when the staffing manager may want to drill down further to understand the drivers of performance. To understand bottom line results, managers must have visibility into the SG&A costs it takes to support different segments of clients and service offerings. This information is valuable when there are segments within a staffing company that require a much higher amount of SG&A to drive the same gross profit as other segments. These segments siphon away from the bottom line, while at the same time leading the managers to believe that their producers are highly productive. An effective manager sees the whole picture and understands the true impact of different businesses on the company's bottom line.

In the following example, we analyze the SG&A costs by Clients A and B. We have already discussed how Client B has a lower revenue stream, but a higher GP% and thus adds more GP$. If we assume total SG&A costs of 20% for both clients, the impact of the lower GP% becomes clearer with Client A actually losing money when you subtract the SG&A costs. With similar SG&A costs, Client B contributes $360 of profit.

ANALYZE GROSS PROFIT AND SG&A BY CLIENT					
Company	Monthly Revenue	Gross Profit Percentage	Gross Profit Earned Monthly	Total SG&A Costs (20%)	Operating Profit/ EBITDA
Client A	$8,000	18%	$1,440	$1,600	($160)
Client B	$6,000	26%	$1,560	$1,200	$360

Many times the SG&A costs are not similar across clients. If you assume Client A has good revenue, low GP% and SG&A costs higher than 20%, then you are losing even more money on this client. VMS clients tend to have low GP% and higher submittal rate, so a careful analysis of the business is in order. Of course VMS can be profitable with the right amount of volume or a low cost per submittal, but it is always good to analyze GP%

and SG&A costs for each individual client.

It is also important to understand the effects of recruiter productivity on SG&A costs. The following chart assumes Recruiter A makes around $8,000 per month and averages 40 submittals per month. A quick calculation reveals that the average cost per submittal is about $200 which is admittedly a bit high, but not unreasonable. If they are working a VMS account that requires 25 submittals to make a single placement then you have spent $5,000 on just recruiting headcount cost to make that placement. With clients that require a large volume of submittals to make a placement, staffing companies must respond with recruiters that can generate those submittals.

RECRUITER COST PER SUBMITTAL					
	Monthly Salary	Submittals /Month	Cost Per Submittal	Submittal-to-Hire	Cost for One Placement
Recruiter A	$8,000	40	$200	25:1	$5,000

It is also important to analyze the submittal-to-hire ratio for each client and compare that to the gross profit generated by that client. In the following chart, we assume Client A has a 25:1 submittal-to-hire ratio while Client B has an 8:1 submittal-to-hire ratio. We will assume that both have $200 cost per submittal based on the compensation numbers in the chart above. As discussed, Client A has a 25:1 submittal-to-hire ratio so it costs $5,000 to hire that one placement. However, they only receive a monthly gross profit of $1,440. Client B has an 8:1 submittal-to-hire ratio, so it costs $1,600 to hire one placement and they will generate $1,560 in gross profit per month.

GROSS PROFIT BY CLIENT				
Company	**Monthly Revenue**	**Gross Profit Percentage**	**Gross Profit Earned Monthly**	**Cost per Submittal**
Client A	$8,000	18%	$1,440	$200
Client B	$6,000	26%	$1,560	$200
COST PER PLACEMENT BY CLIENT				
Company	**Gross Profit Percentage**	**Submittal/ Hire Ratio**	**Cost per Submittal**	**Cost per Placement**
Client A	18%	25/1	$200	$5,000
Client B	26%	8/1	$200	$1,600

The impact of the submittal-to-hire ratio is revealed when you compare the recovery period of the two clients. It takes four months to recover the submittal costs of the placement for Client A, while the submittal costs are basically covered in one month for Client B.

Recovery Period for Submittal Costs

Client A

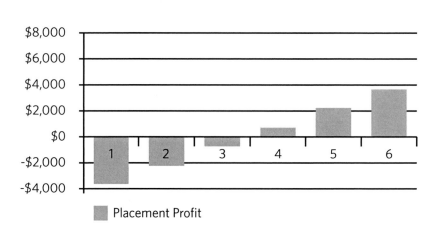

Placement Profit

Client B

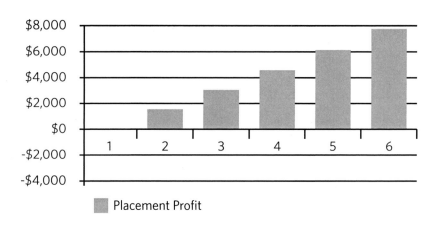

Placement Profit

Keep in mind the previous examples only take into account staff compensation when calculating cost per submittal. If you also consider other sales costs, job boards, and office space, you will see how quickly the submittal-to-hire ratio can drag down the bottom line. To make matters worse, many clients who have high submittal-to-hire ratios also have low gross profits impacting profitability from both sides of the equation. If you find yourself in a scenario where your submittal-to-hire ratios vary significantly between accounts or even among account managers, you should drill down to see how it is impacting your bottom line.

In addition to the varying costs associated with each client, different business models will also impact SG&A costs. With a branch model, there are increased costs associated with leasing each office, more management expense, as well as higher IT and office equipment costs. In most cases with a centralized model, the cost per person should be lower since there is only one location, presumably less management costs, and decreased overall office costs. This is not to say that everyone should switch to a centralized model. The branch model is definitely beneficial for diversifying your client base, but you must weigh the incremental costs of adding each location.

You will also need to weigh the impact to SG&A costs of adding each new recruiter or sales person. If you assume that your physical location can support adding one more employee, then you will need to calculate the cost of their salary, benefits, licensing, training, and office equipment such as a computer, phone, etc. You will also need the cash flow to support these expenses until the new employee begins making placements. The following graph shows an example of expenses and income for a new recruiter in the first six months.

Expenses vs. Gross Profit of a New Recruiter

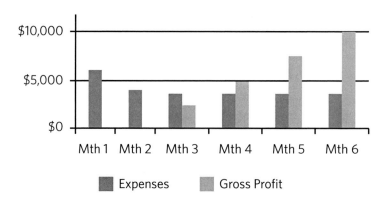

Comparing the costs versus the potential gross profit that one employee can contribute is a great indicator of the low barriers to entry within this industry. However, before you hire lots of new employees, you will need to analyze whether your organization can support the additional bandwidth, as well as the cash flow necessary to fund them for at least the first six months.

Performance Drivers and Financial Results

In addition to the tangible costs of employees and offices, the sales strategy, operational alignment, and the Performance-Driven Culture also impact financial results. A staffing company which has healthy drivers across the board will experience growth above their peers and tend to have an increased level of profitability. In order to fully understand the impact of each of the drivers, this section will discuss how each of them uniquely impacts financial results.

The sales strategy directly impacts all levels of financial results. From top-line growth to bottom-line profitability, there is no escaping the relationship between the sales strategy and the financial health of the company. The pervasiveness of the sales strategy's impact is due to one simple rule:

> *A staffing organization is largely defined both operationally and financially by the clients it chooses to support.*

Regardless of what strategy the executive team has laid out and what delivery model they have built, I can understand more about the state of an organization by looking at the current book of business. This can lead to conflict with executives who believe they have built a different company than their book of business reveals. This is especially true for companies that define their differentiator on quality, but support national VMS accounts. The two simply cannot coexist.

The following bullet points are some areas of the financials that can be directly impacted by the sales strategy.

- Growth accounts drive year over year top-line performance.
- High GP% accounts lead to greater bottom-line profitability.
- Productive accounts with high close rates reduce the need for high SG&A investments.
- Strong sales strategy drives gross profit diversification.
- Healthy GP% and payment terms improve cash flow, reduce the need for credit, and provide investment dollars for growth.

While there are some similarities on the impact of operational align-ment on financials, it all must begin with a healthy client base. Operation-al alignment can help maximize the growth of current accounts, but that growth will slow down and eventually stop if a strong sales strategy is not in place. On the flip side, if the sales team builds a healthy client base, then delivery can quickly become the bottleneck if they cannot follow through on the value proposition. Assuming a well-executed sales strategy, the po-tential financial impact of strong operational alignment includes:

- Top-line growth through account penetration.
- Increased submittal throughput requiring lower recruiter-to-sales ra-tio, reducing headcount investment.
- Greater productivity per producer leading to stronger bottom line re-sults.
- Potential reduction on the reliance of job boards leading to greater sav-ings on SG&A expenses.

While it is easy to understand the impact of the sales strategy and operational alignment on financial results, the impact of the performance culture might not seem as clear. Because staffing is a people-driven busi-ness, how people are motivated to work together has a direct impact on financial results.

- Hiring profiles determine initial investment for new employees.

- Hiring, performance management and training ensure poor producers are kept at a minimum, thus improving gross profit per producer.

- Compensation levels determine the amount of gross profit paid out as compensation impacting SG&A.

- A motivated team that effectively collaborates is a factor that impacts both top and bottom-line growth.

Wrapping Up

In the end, while each driver impacts financial results in distinct ways, the most important point to remember is that they are all interdependent. A strong sales strategy needs strong operations to take advantage of the demand it creates. At the same time, the Performance-Driven Culture motivates individuals to work as a team to maximize the opportunities in front of them. A staffing organization with strength in all three drivers will see healthy financial growth, while others will only grow as much as the weakest driver will allow.

Chapter 5:
From Theory to Practice

We have just discussed how the three drivers – sales strategy, operational alignment and Performance-Driven Culture – determine a staffing company's financial results. Understanding these three drivers is just the first step in more effective management. Now it is time for you, as a manager, to use your best judgment on how to apply them. The style, timing, and accuracy will contribute to your entire team's performance.

This chapter recommends a four-step approach:

- Define Your Growth Strategy
- Build Your Metrics Portfolio
- Develop a Governance Plan
- Execute and Adapt.

While this sounds like a straightforward approach, it does not mean it is simple. Strategy is the base point of all activity, so we will start there.

Define Your Growth Strategy

The term "strategy" is one of those words that mean different things to different people. In this chapter, we use this definition:

Strategy: The growth plan defined by executives along with the critical operational elements that provide the company its competitive edge.

We introduced the following graph in Chapter 1, but it is important to keep the relationship with each of these three drivers on the financial results in mind when determining strategy.

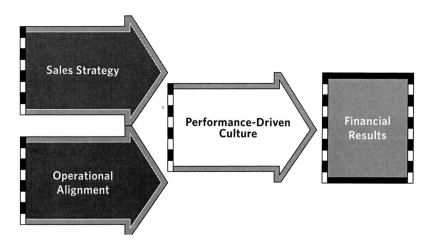

Following is a list of questions to clarify the relationship between defining a company strategy and the performance model. These questions may or may not be entirely relevant in evaluating and redefining your company's strategy.

Financial Results

- Will growth be driven organically?
- Where will top-line growth come from and how much should we expect?
- What type of gross margins should we expect?
- What level of SG&A is required?
- What level of profit should we expect?
- What are the cash flow dynamics?
- Are there any areas within the financials that must be a top priority to improve?

Sales Strategy

- Who should be our target buyers?
- What should be our unique value proposition?
- How should we define our offerings to capture that value?
- What sales activities should occur for the sales strategy to be successful?

Operational Alignment

- How should requirements be qualified before they enter the queue?
- What criteria should be used to prioritize requirements?
- How should requirements be assigned to the recruiting team?
- How should we enable sourcing?
- How should we manage our candidate inventory?

Performance-Driven Culture

- What level of experience do our people need to execute the strategy?
- What ongoing training is required?

- How should we measure and manage producers to ensure they are driving the right activities?
- How should we compensate to encourage the right behaviors?
- What other incentives would motivate the team?

Answering these questions provides the initial growth roadmap for the organization. This roadmap features both the desired financial model along with an initial understanding of how all the drivers must improve to accomplish the financial goals. Now that you understand and have come to terms with the scope of change required, the next thing is to further define the strategy in operational terms by developing strategic objectives.

Objectives

Objectives provide a strong foundation by ensuring the growth strategy is defined in operational terms that can be measured and managed. When developing objectives you should take into account the following:

- Define the required capabilities of each strategic driver.
- Identify high impact improvements required to achieve those capabilities.

These two components provide the blueprint for future growth. The objectives clearly detail management's responsibility to drive the strategy by first defining the organization's current capabilities and then detail the actions management must actively improve for the strategy to be successful. This blueprint provides management the insight to balance the day-to-day problems with improvements needed for sustainable long-term growth.

Financial Objectives

When developing an objective-based management system, you should always begin with financial objectives. Financial objectives represent the desired results of the strategy and should be defined accordingly. Examples of financial objectives are:

- Improve top-line growth
- Improve profitability
- Diversify financial model
- Improve net income
- Improve gross profit percentage
- Improve ROI.

Keep in mind, these financial objectives are the areas that the organization must either show mastery in or significantly change to say the strategy has been successful. These objectives are not meant to replace the other financial statements, but instead to focus the organization on a few easy-to-understand results. With that in mind, you should choose three or four financial objectives using the questions outlined earlier in the chapter as a guide.

Assume we have a staffing company whose primary strategic issues are client diversification and profitability. In this case, they would want to choose financial objectives that directly address these significant long-term threats to the business. Objectives they would develop could include:

- Improve profitability
- Increase EBITDA
- Increase gross profit growth.

These financial objectives represent the intended results of the strategy. These reflect what the operations must do to meet those goals. Operational objectives must be defined beginning with the sales strategy.

Sales Strategy Objectives

Objectives for the sales strategy should focus on three or four important activities that the sales organization must master to drive the desired financial results. Sales strategy objectives center on how the sales process drives the value proposition to bring in the right book of business from the target accounts. Unlike financial objectives that focus on results, many of the sales objectives should be leading indicators of the strategy to give management a forward-looking perspective of how the organization is transforming.

Using the same sample company, some sales objectives may include:

- Improve account diversification
- Improve placement profitability
- Improve job order quality.

Operational Alignment Objectives

Once the objectives around the sales strategy are defined, the next step is to define the objectives around operational alignment. Operational alignment focuses on the critical processes from the time a job order enters the organization to the time a candidate is placed on assignment. These processes include:

- Job order qualification
- Job order prioritization
- Job order assignment
- Sourcing
- Submittal management.

As in the sales strategy, only three or four objectives should be developed. It is possible that some processes can be ignored while others have more than one objective. Choosing which processes receive the most attention should be based on the strategy and the unique delivery capabilities that are required to drive that strategy. When considering objectives around operational alignment, it often makes sense to consider measurement on responsiveness, quality, and submittal throughput. For example, a staffing company that focuses on VMS may be more concerned with responsiveness and quantity measures than a branch driven staffing company.

Some operational alignment objectives that could make sense for our sample company include:

- Improve candidate quality
- Increase sourcing capabilities
- Improve coverage to prospects.

Performance-Driven Culture Objectives

The final set of objectives that need to be defined surround the Performance-Driven Culture. These objectives focus on key activities that ensure the right people are hired, retained, and motivated. Finding measurable objectives can be difficult in this area since culture itself is in many ways subjective. Also, it is important to consider that these objectives are sup-plemented by a strong performance management system for individuals.

Some Performance-Driven Culture objectives that our sample compa-ny may consider include:

- Improve internal hiring
- Strengthen sales training
- Improve ATS utilization.

Objectives such as improving ATS utilization may not seem cultural, but these objectives make the assumption that a successful employee is a motivated employee. Therefore anything that directly enables the success of individuals can reasonably be considered as part of Performance-Driven Culture objectives.

Build Your Metrics Portfolio

Now that you have defined your strategic objectives, the next step is to build a metrics portfolio to ensure those objectives will be met. A met-rics portfolio is made up of both measures and the targets that provide the benchmark for performance levels.

Management teams have the most heated discussions while develop-ing measurements for the objectives. This is the time when the objectives are truly defined for these three reasons:

1. Define Behaviors: The measures help define what the objective means to the management team. "Diversify account base," for ex-ample, is an objective that the majority of staffing firms would want

to accomplish. The measures you choose define what the management team thinks are the behaviors necessary to meet that objective.

For example, a staffing company focusing on large national programs with an objective to diversify the client base may choose to measure activity around RFPs. In contrast, a boutique firm who avoids those programs may choose to measure placements made at new accounts. It is this type of distinction that truly defines and brings clarity to the strategic drivers. Confronted with this clarity, the management team must now get on the same page to plot how the strategy is adopted with the operations. This challenge may lead to healthy, but often lengthy disagreements.

2. Define Improvements: The measures you choose define the capability gaps the management team will focus on. It is important to keep in mind that most organizations have multiple gaps. The question is whether management is focusing on the right gaps. The metrics portfolio must capture the critical bottlenecks that are inhibiting growth. Ongoing management attention to this issue is crucial. Too often management spends energy on what is urgent and what they can tolerate, and delay dealing with what is really important. Measures allow them to stay focused on the right activities.

A manager focusing on urgent problems and management complacency are the most common roadblocks to management development. This combination allows managers to believe they are being productive by staying busy. I have seen senior VPs fall into this trap, stunting both the company's as well as their own professional growth.

3. <u>Define Roles:</u> The measures you choose help clarify the job descriptions for the management team. These measures capture what success looks like. Management then takes that vision and adapts how they manage the business on a day-to-day basis. It also defines what improvement initiatives management must implement to ensure that they fill critical performance gaps. These measures become the language of the management team by clearly defining the terms of success and failure.

Now that you understand the importance of picking the right measurements, you need to decide on the types of measurements. A metrics portfolio should have measures that balance visibility into business-as-usual performance, as well as the progress on the change initiatives that are taking place. This balance can be achieved by ensuring you have the following measures:

- Activity measures
- Result measures
- Change measures.

Activity and result measures focus on the execution of today's business while change measures ensure that long-term improvements are taking hold. Activity measures typically are viewed as leading indicators that focus on the beginning of the pipeline of business. Result metrics are dominated by lagging indicators whose role is to ensure the strategy is leading to the right outcomes. Both activity and result metrics can be viewed as a point in time or as a long-term trend. Change measures always should be seen as leading indicators of the future state of the organization and should track progress over a period of time.

Each objective should have at least one measure, and ideally no more than two. If you cannot think of a measure or you need more than two measures for the objective, you need to change the objective. Objectives that have no measure are meaningless from a management perspective and objectives with more than two are cumbersome. When developing measures, remember that they need to be simple, yet comprehensive.

Achieving a proper balance between the objectives and measures will go a long way in developing a user-friendly yet effective measurement system. Following is a chart showing the relationship between objectives and measures. These are examples only and are not meant to be considered "best practices."

OBJECTIVE	MEASURE
Financial Results	
Improve Profitability	Contract GM%
Increase EBITDA	% Growth Year over Year
Increase Gross Profit Growth	% Growth Year over Year
Sales Strategy	
Improve Account Diversification	# Placements at New Accounts
Improve Placement Profitability	Avg Week GP of New Placements
Increase Account Manager Productivity	% of AMs Hitting Goal
Operational Alignment	
Improve Candidate Quality	% of Internal Submittals Sent to Clients
Increase Sourcing Capabilities	# of Candidates Added to ATS
Improve Coverage to Prospects	% of Prospect JOs with 2 or More Submittals
Performance-Driven Culture	
Improve Internal Hiring	% of New Hires Completing 60-Day Plan
Strengthen Sales Training	# of Sales Training Events

After the objectives and measures are put into place, it is time to determine your target metrics. When defining targets, it is important to review industry standards as well past operational trends. When evaluating industry standard benchmarks, financial reporting tends to be more useful than operational or performance metrics. This could be due to the fact that accurate financial reporting is legally required, and the people who are responsible for generating this reporting, such as the CFO or controller, are specifically trained to provide this information. External studies on financial benchmarks such as revenue growth, gross profit percentage, SG&A costs, and profitability using industry standards provide accurate and important insight.

When using industry benchmarks around operational and performance metrics, you need to be more judicious. The data from these studies tends to be less reliable for a few reasons, but primarily because most firms do not track the data they do not manage. This lack of ongoing tracking impacts ATS compliance making the data less reliable. Also, the managers responsible for reporting the front office data are more likely to estimate the numbers than the back office such as the CFO or controller. Unfortunately, most managers who guess typically overestimate team performance around a metric they do not manage.

As a general rule, the data at the beginning of the funnel is the least accurate and the data closer towards the placement tends to be more accurate. When developing targets, you can use past performance for front-end activity such as cold calls, meetings, and screenings. Leverage external data for metrics that are closer to results including job orders, submittals, interviews, and placements

Once you have defined the objectives, measures, and targets, much of the foundation of the management system is in place. The management team has already defined the financial model along with the operational capabilities required to achieve the desired results. The next step is to identify and prioritize the improvement initiatives that must take place. Improvement initiatives are projects whose primary purpose is to bridge the gap between objective targets and actual performance. Initiatives have a beginning and end date, a budget, and an owner. Some examples of initiatives are:

- Develop new marketing material
- Determine job board ROI
- Add recruiting headcount
- Develop new sales reporting for prospecting.

Each of these initiatives should have an owner who is responsible for ensuring the project is completed by the intended end date. Owners of initiatives typically are part of the management team, and manage over an area that is directly impacted by the initiative. For example, the initiative of determining job board ROI would be headed up by an operations or recruiting manager.

Develop the Governance Plan

As we discussed in Chapter 1, governance is the definition of the management roles and the approach managers take to effectively execute those roles. How those roles are defined and executed is driven by the growth strategy and the metrics portfolio to manage it.

The objectives, measures, and targets, along with the initiatives, provide the foundation of the governance plan. They define what management must focus on, and how they are going to hold themselves accountable as leaders. Now the question to be answered is how management must behave differently to drive the strategy. The first step in answering this question is refining management roles.

MANAGEMENT ROLES

At the most basic level, there is a lot a manager must effectively do to manage the status quo of the business. These responsibilities should still be documented as part of each manager's role including:

- Motivate the team
- Be an example of company values
- Provide ongoing coaching
- Effectively address internal conflicts
- Act as an escalation point for clients
- Provide executive's insight on operational trends
- Ensure compliance with company policies
- Hire capable personnel.

Traditionally, managers in the staffing industry are left to their own devices to figure out all the above items. This can work in situations where the manager is exceptionally talented and where the operations are not required to undergo any significant improvements. But even the most gifted managers struggle with the ability to drive improvements within their organization. Defining the management role through the lenses of the objectives and the initiatives provides important insight into the skills and abilities required to drive the business to its desired state.

> *Two rules of strategic execution must be applied when evaluating management roles:*
> - *Operations will not change without intentional leadership from management.*
> - *The ability to drive the changes and improvements necessary to successfully execute a strategy primarily is limited by the skills, bandwidth, and discipline of the management team.*

How management roles are defined is determined by structure. In organizations with only one manager over the entire operation, they are responsible for all the objectives. In this situation, the scope of change may need to remain narrow, depending on the maturity of the production team.

Organizations with multiple managers must assign accountability under each objective. For example, sales managers would be directly accountable for all sales process objectives and potentially some objectives around job order management. Recruiting managers are held accountable for delivery objectives, and in some cases are held accountable for lead generation to drive the sales process. For the most part, the entire management team has a part in driving the financial and Performance-Driven Culture objectives.

MANAGEMENT ROLES AND CHANGE

One of the most common mistakes executives make is to choose a shift in the firm's financial model – but not define the operational terms that are responsible for making that new model a reality. For small shifts in the strategy that require incremental change, overlooking this step may or may not be detrimental. Execution of the strategy will suffer, but strong individual performers and a bit of luck can overcome the headwinds created by a poorly defined strategy.

Some examples where the strategy may require only incremental change include:

- New, high-profile role
- Change in compensation plans
- Minor technology investments
- New branch or division.

While these changes may require different levels of investments, they can be considered relatively minor from a change management perspective because the existing performance drivers escape relatively unscathed. These strategic decisions remain within the core capabilities of the performance drivers, reducing the likelihood and the overall impact of failure on the organization.

However, there are other strategies that require transformational adjustments to the performance drivers. Organizations choose these strategies for a variety of reasons. Some have existing clients asking them to increase their capabilities or they see a clear path to gain market share. While these are positive reasons for transformational change, too often these strategies are developed in periods of duress. The most common example is staffing companies who must regain their sales edge after becoming delivery organizations. This is a very difficult transformation that often determines the ongoing existence of a staffing company. These types of strategies provide the greatest challenges to the management team.

Some strategic decisions that often require transformational change include:

- Change in value proposition (new service offering)
- Merger or acquisition
- Changing target buyers
- Massive restructuring of sales and delivery processes
- Transformational technology (New ATS/CRM)
- Large scale organizational restructuring.

Executives often underestimate the time, skill, and monetary investment required to drive transformational change. Many strategies fail because the managers do not appreciate the level of oversight required to see the strategy implemented.

The following chart can give you a better appreciation for the scope of change required to fully implement a strategy. Since the scope of change required is different for each company, you can use the chart to mark T for transformational, I for incremental, and NC for no change based on your company.

FINANCIAL	SCOPE OF CHANGE
Source of Revenue/GM	
Change in Profitability	
Scope of New SG&A Investments	
Sales Strategy	**Scope of Change**
Service Offerings	
Penetrating Existing Accounts	
Landing New Accounts	
Operational Alignment	**Scope of Change**
Sourcing	
Job Order Qualification	
Job Order Management	
Job Order Prioritization	
Candidate Quality	
Submittal Management	
Performance-Driven Culture	**Scope of Change**
Hiring/Onboarding	
Compensation Plans/ Incentives	
Performance Management	
Organizational Structure	

If your strategy requires multiple areas to undergo transformational change and/or those areas are focused within one driver, then you must ask yourself three questions concerning the management team:

- Does my team have the skill to lead change of this scope and complexity?
- Do my managers have the available time to actively manage the transformation?
- How big is the impact to the core business if my managers focus on the improvements necessary for the new strategy?

It is difficult for a manager to know for certain whether they are trying to change an organization too much, but the first step is an honest assessment of the impact in each of the strategic drivers. In general, if you look at the scope of change required of the management team and you have a pit in your stomach, then trust your instincts and pull back. The worst thing an executive can do is roll out a change initiative that is too large in scope to manage. These types of change initiatives are not only built to fail, but they also undermine productivity and the reputation of management leaving the organization worse off than if things were just left alone.

MANAGEMENT APPROACH

Once the management roles are defined, then the next step is to discuss how management must work together to govern the business more effectively. Meetings are a critical component of this process. There are three kinds of meetings that management should hold to govern the business: operations meetings, scorecard meetings, and performance management meetings.

The Operations Meeting focuses on short-term performance and initiatives. In these meetings, management will discuss leading indicators that impact financial performance and discuss any tactical housekeeping issues. These meetings are often weekly, but can be monthly depending on the organization.

The Scorecard Meeting focuses primarily on the progress of the objectives and improvement initiatives. In these meetings, the owners of each of the objectives and initiatives report on the progress against target metrics and deadlines. If objectives are not being met, then the team uses this time to discuss the reasons for nonperformance and the legitimacy of the strategic assumptions. Unlike the operations meeting, the scorecard meeting is meant to measure progress over time. For this reason, the meetings are done on either a monthly or quarterly basis.

The Performance Management Meeting focuses on individual producers. It is important to remember that staffing is a people-driven business. For that reason, you must set aside time to conduct meaningful performance reviews for individual employees. These performance reviews should be either monthly or quarterly, and focus on metrics that are aligned with the objectives. When developing your metrics systems for sales and recruiting personnel, you should have measures of activity, quality, and results.

- Activity focuses on highly controllable metrics that drive results. Some example of activity metrics include: calls, meetings, and submittals.
- Quality metrics measure the productivity of the activity the producer generates. Quality metrics are typically ratios such as submittal-to-hire.
- Result metrics focus on the end result of the activity. Some examples of result metrics include: hires, gross profit dollars, and billable consultants.

The management team must have well-defined roles and a clear plan of action to drive performance in their organization. By having both of these elements, managers will collaborate more effectively with one another as well as their production team to meet the short and long-term objectives of the company's growth strategy.

Execute and Adapt

When I am approached by a staffing company to consult, one of the first things I want to know is their size. The reason for this is simple. The size of the organization determines where management should focus and what type of management framework they need.

Startups and small staffing firms should have performance management in place with a very simple sales and recruiting process. As organizations get bigger, their management framework must become more comprehensive, especially when multiple management layers are introduced. Staffing managers may be tempted to implement multiple ideas from this book, but that may not be necessary. Instead of blind adoption, ask yourself three questions:

- *Does the idea break open a significant bottleneck?*
- *Do I have the time, expertise, and discipline to follow through?*
- *Am I overcomplicating the solution or can it be simplified?*

Once a management team begins to manage differently, they will soon see the organization in a new light. The greater visibility and increased accountability will improve management team collaboration. For those managers new to this level of management structure, be prepared for a good bit of frustration.

The first phase of frustration is gathering accurate data. Management teams who have not been measuring their operations will soon find out that their systems are little used and that their data is inaccurate. They will then have to reconfigure their tools and retrain their teams to ensure they have the visibility they need to drive the business.

The second phase of frustration is realizing the inaccuracy of your assumptions. The data will reveal ugly truths within your operations and may show weaknesses that you thought were strengths. Many managers have a difficult time with this phase as they realize how much work really needs to be done to strengthen the organization.

The third phase of frustration is the slow pace of change. Staffing by nature is a fast moving, impatient business. Change is slow and requires ongoing focus and energy. However long you think a change initiative should take, double it, and then you probably need to double it again to envision an accurate duration.

While these frustrations are real, they are only a reflection of past fabrications. Managers must ground themselves in reality, see what needs to be improved, and act decisively and with conviction. Understanding the drivers within a staffing operation is the first step. The more difficult step of changing how your organization manages requires honest reflection, strong leadership, discipline, and persistence.

Wrapping Up

Executives must take the first step in putting these concepts to work by developing a well-defined, objective-based growth strategy. These objectives must be measurable, providing the foundation of a metrics portfolio that is balanced, focused, and comprehensive.

The real test of the strategy is making sure the management team has the skills, time, and discipline to implement the improvements without negatively impacting the core business. This is done effectively by defining each management role through the lens of the objectives. Management must then determine the approach they will take in managing the business both within their individual roles and as an entire team.

Management must also be willing to adapt in order for their organization to survive the growing competitive forces. As the execution of the strategy takes place problems will arise. Management must adapt their approach to address those problems and in some cases be willing to challenge the strategy.

Conclusion

Start-up staffing companies typically are strong sales organizations with unwavering dedication to their clients. Many staffing companies stop at this stage. They top out in the $10 million range and they continue to manage their business the same way as when they began. In this changing marketplace, even these staffing companies must take the viewpoint that they must adapt or die. This pursuit of improvement is not just about revenue and net income, but growing the competitive capabilities of the organization knowing that your competitors are doing the same. Moving beyond the small-scale relationship to a well-aligned staffing organization that has a strong sales strategy, scalable operations, and a competitive Performance-Driven Culture is a difficult but necessary step.

Embracing the concepts within this book is not just about growing faster than the market or even maintaining your current size. Instead, these management concepts are integral for the long-term survival of any staffing company. Regardless of size, vertical, or geography, the same competitive forces from buyers, suppliers, and other factors will continue to put pressure on your operations. Only strong, disciplined managers will be able to navigate through this competitive marketplace and ensure their company not only survives, but thrives in both the short and long-term.

The ability to chart and lead a path for the entire organization is management's primary responsibility. This is also its greatest contribution to those they lead and one they are obligated to master. My hope is that this book at least provides you with the scope of your stewardship and helps empower you and your team to build something exceptional. Our employees, clients, and contractors deserve nothing less.

Acknowledgements

I woud like to acknowledge the following people for their support and inspiration:

Marilee Cleland, Bonnie Daneker, Carrie Wallace Brown, David Findley, Brad Mencher, Bill Gower, Bill Solon, Ed Lewis, Richard Zambacca, Eric French, Sandra Anderson, Melissa Davis, Ella Koscik, Amy Vasquez, Ed Barrows, Richey Brownfield, Ruben Santana, Mark Roberts, Al Dubuc, Leslie Vickery, Sona Sharma, Barry Asin, Mark Roberts, Susan Donahue, John Cloonan, Monique Honaman, Don and Marilyn Cleland, Dr. D. B. Shelnutt.

The organizations that support our industry: TechServe Alliance, American Staffing Association, Staffing Industry Analyst.

The partners who support my clients: Bullhorn, Haley Marketing, ClearEdge Marketing, TempWorks, Debellas and Co., CareerBuilder, Monster, Childs Advisory Partners, LinkedIn, and eRecruit.

About the Author

Mike has over 19 years' experience in the staffing industry. Since the founding of Charted Path in February 2010, he has facilitated solutions with executives, owners, and investors for over 45 companies in multiple staffing verticals, including IT, engineering, healthcare, light industrial, clerical, legal, and managed services, with revenues ranging from $10 million to $200 million. Solutions have included, but not limited to:

- Strategic Planning
- Management Workshop Facilitation
- Management Development
- Sales and Recruiting Process Improvement
- Performance Management Improvement
- Compensation Plan Development
- Front Office Tool Selection and Configuration
- Metrics Portfolio Creation.

Throughout his career, Mike's commitment to continuous improvement to stay ahead of market changes played a crucial role as a producer, line level manager, executive, and consultant.

In the early nineties, Mike led key initiatives to improve recruiting performance such as reorganizing the recruiting team to improve competitiveness, rolling out the first website and incorporating automation into the recruiting process.

A few years later, Mike opened the first remote office for his company in the Carolinas where he conducted the market research, identified and hired local talent, developed a customized recruiting and CRM tool for the market. Mike built a strong, well-diversified book of business which still maintains above industry average gross margins.

As an enterprise-wide manager, Mike focused on driving improvements across the entire organization. These improvements included increasing productivity by over 30% through automation and effective job order management, centralizing and scaling partnership program to increase delivery capabilities, and developing and implementing new compensation plans to drive growth and profitability.

As an executive, Mike led the effort in the evaluation, creation and execution of company strategy leveraging Kaplan and Norton's Strategy Map and Balanced Scorecard methodology. Mike then led efforts in marketing rebranding, sales process redesign, CRM tool implementation, and the development of modular sales training.

To learn more about Mike Cleland or sign-up for his newsletter, visit his website at www.chartedpath.com. If you have any questions, feel free to email Mike at questions@chartedpath.com.

Glossary

To best use this book, you will need to understand the key terms and conventions which are described below.

Account Planning: A process focusing on developing account plans.

Active Management: Formal process where management actively determines job order management.

Activity Metrics: Metrics focusing on activity volume.

Assets: Anything of value in the company including cash or anything that can be converted into cash.

Assignment Management: Process of managing current contractor staff.

Attrition Rate: The average turnover rate of contractor staff.

Balance Sheet: Captures the financial state of the company at a point in time through the perspective of assets, liabilities, and owners' equity.

Bill Rate Chart: Rate chart structured by not to exceed bill rates.

Bonus: Flat amount paid on specific events.

Bottleneck: An operational inefficiency so significant that is acts as the primary restriction to growth.

Branch Model: Staffing company structure focusing on local market presence.

Burdened Cost: The statutory and compensation costs of employing a contractor.

Business Developer: A sales role focusing on landing new accounts.

Buyer Matrix: Captures the four buyer types the staffing manager will encounter in the market.

Buyer: Company that uses contingent labor.

Candidate Qualification: The process of qualifying a candidate for a specific opportunity.

Cash Flow Statement: Captures the flow of cash in and out of the business.

Centralized Model: Staffing company structure focusing on wide geographical support from centralized centers.

Client Base: List of billing accounts.

Compelling Event: Business event that drives contract spend.

Cost Per Submittal: Recruiting costs per number of submittals.

Culture: Unwritten rules that drive behavior within an organization.

Customer Service: Staffing value proposition focusing on high quality service to both clients and consultants.

Delivery Manager: A manager responsible for job order and submittal management.

EBITDA: A good measure of the bottom line an operation earns by subtracting direct and operational costs from the revenue line. Does not take into account interest, taxes, depreciation and amortizations.

Executive Summary: Summary of candidates' qualifications for a specific position.

False Start: Candidate accepts the position but never starts.

Governance Plan: The compilation of all management roles, how those roles interact, and manage the business as a team.

Governance: The distinct roles managers have and the approach to those roles.

Gross Profit: Financial line item that captures the bill rate minus the burdened cost of the contractor. The most accurate measure of top-line growth often used in performance management and compensation.

Growth Strategy: A growth plan based on desired results and strategic drivers.

Hiring Authority: A manager's ability to influence the process of hiring talent from agencies.

Hiring Manager: Direct decision maker on hiring contingent labor.

Hiring Process: The steps and personnel associated with a client's hiring process.

Income Statement: A financial statement that shows the relationship between revenue, expenses, and the bottom line over a specified period of time.

Initiative: A strategic improvement project.

Internal Submittal: The recruiter submits a candidate to another internal resource before it is sent to the client.

Interview-to-Hire: Calculated by dividing number of interviews by those hired. A measure of candidate or job order quality.

Job Order Assignment: The process of how jobs are assigned recruiting resources.

Job Order Management: The processes that focus on how job orders are managed within the organization.

Job Order Prioritization: The process of managing a job orders priority within the job order queue.

Job Order Qualification: The process of qualifying a job order based on an objective set or criteria.

Job Order Queue: The population of jobs that are being worked by the company at any point in time.

Joint Sales Call: A strategic meeting including a buyer, staffing manager, and a sales person.

Key Decision Maker (KDM): An individual who determines or influences the decision of who is added to the vendor list.

Laissez-Faire: Informal process where the production team determines job order management.

Lead: Buyer information that identifies a specific opportunity or market intelligence.

Liabilities: Financial obligations the company has from prior transactions.

Management framework: The overall structure of the management approach including the growth strategy, metrics portfolio, and the governance plan.

Mark Up Percentage: Rate chart structured by a percentage markup of contractor's compensation.

Market Intelligence: A lead that provides general information that is useful to understanding a company's buying patterns.

Metrics Portfolio: The entire portfolio of data that informs management of critical business trends.

MSP: Managed Service Provider is an organization that manages staffing programs for buyers.

Objective: A measurable success factor in a company's strategy.

Off: A contractor who has finished their assignment.

On-boarding: The work necessary to prepare a newly hired candidate.

Operational Alignment: A strategic driver that focuses on delivery.

Operational Metrics: Metrics that provide insight into the health of an entire operation.

Opportunity: A lead that provides information around specific managers hiring for specific positions.

Override: Variable compensation determined by a percentage of a financial result.

Owner's Equity: Individual shareholder interest in the company.

Passive Candidates: Candidates who do not post their resumes on public boards.

Perception of Service: How a hiring manager views staffing providers.

Performance Metrics: Metrics focusing on individual performance.

Performance Review: One-on-one performance review between direct management and producer.

Performance-Driven Culture: Culture where performance is defined and naturally driven.

Quality Metrics: Metrics focusing on return of activity.

Quality: The details of job orders and candidates that generate a quality match.

Recruiting Model: The defined delivery processes to fill jobs.

Requirements: All required elements of a position a candidate must meet.

Responsiveness: The speed of delivery processes.

Rogue Spend: Ways hiring managers can fund contract labor outside a staffing program.

Rules of Engagement: Rules of vendor behavior for staffing programs.

Sales Objectives: Measureable success factors for the sales organization.

Sales Process: The defined activities that sales force must execute to drive value proposition to target buyers.

Sales Strategy: A strategic driver that focuses on market strategy.

SG&A Costs: The direct costs of running the operation. Is broken up into sales, general, and administrative costs. Some things included in SG&A are salaries, facilities costs, commissions, and benefits of internal employees.

Skills: Specific abilities required by job orders.

Solution Bias: Tendency of a manager to implement the same solution based on past experience.

Sourcing: The process of building pools of candidates and the different means of communication to contact those pools.

Specialization: Staffing value proposition that separates itself through quality by specialization.

Speed, Price, Scale: A type of staffing value proposition.

Staffing Program: Any formalized program a buyer uses to manage contingent labor spending.

Staffing: Service that focuses on providing contingent labor.

Statement of Work (SOW): A way to finance projects traditionally through fixed billings.

Strategic Improvement Metrics: Metrics that provide trending data to show the progress of strategic operational improvements.

Submittal Management: The processes involved in qualifying and placing candidates.

Submittal-to-Client: Process of sending a candidate to a client.

Submittal-to-Hire: Critical efficiency measurement that is impacted by multiple variables.

Suitability: Candidate that fits with the client's culture.

Target Accounts: The type of accounts that the sales force intentionally targets.

Throughput: Volume of work an operation can generate with competitive quality.

Turn Down: Offer turned down by candidate.

Value Proposition: The unique differentiator of a staffing company that compels buyers to purchase from them.

Variable Compensation: Performance based compensation.

VMS: Vendor Management System is a tool buyers use to manage formalized staffing programs.

Workforce Management Solutions: Staffing value proposition providing solutions for the management of buyer's contingent labor.

Bibliography

Articles and Books

Cichelli, David. *Compensating the Sales Force: A practical guide to designing winning sales reward programs*, McGraw-Hill, 2010

Croner, Christopher and Abraham, Richard. *Never Hire a Bad Salesperson Again: Selecting Candidates Who Are Absolutely Driven to Succeed*, The Richard Abraham Company, LLC; 2006

Kaplan, Robert S. and Norton, David P. *The Execution Premium: Linking Strategy to Operations for Competitive Advantage*, Harvard Business School Publishing Corporation, 2008

Kaplan, Robert S. and Norton, David P. *The Strategy-Focused Organization: How Balanced Scorecard Companies Thrive in the New Business Environment*, Harvard Business School Publishing Corporation, 2001

Porter, Michael. "How Competitive Forces Shape Strategy," *Harvard Business Review*, March 3, 2009

Schmidt, Frank L. and Hunter, John E., "The Validity and Utility of Selection Methods in Personnel Psychology: Practical and theoretical implications after 85 years of research findings," American Psychological Association, 1998

Zoltners, Andris A., Sinha, Prabhakant and Lorimer, Salley E. *Building a Winning Sales Force: Powerful Strategies for Driving High Performance*, AMCOM, 2009

Studies
Towers Watson, 2010 Global Workforce Study, 2010

Ray, Rebecca and Rizzacasa, Tom. "Job Satisfaction Survey," The Conference Board, 2011

Film
"Remember the Titans," Walt Disney Pictures, 2000